Tales
from the
Glass
Ceiling

**A Survival Guide
for Women in Business**

Tales
from the
Glass
Ceiling

JO HAIGH

piatkus

PIATKUS

First published in Great Britain in 2008 by Piatkus Books
Reprinted 2008 (twice)
This paperback edition published in 2009 by Piatkus

A CIP catalogue record for this book
is available from the British Library

ISBN 978-0-7499-2957-2

Typeset in Minion by Goldust Design
Printed and bound in Great Britain by Clays Ltd, Bungay, Suffolk

Papers used by Piatkus are natural, renewable and recyclable
products sourced from well-managed forests and certified
in accordance with the rules of the Forest Stewardship Council.

Mixed Sources
Product group from well-managed
forests and other controlled sources
www.fsc.org Cert no. SGS-COC-004081
© 1996 Forest Stewardship Council

Piatkus
An imprint of
Little, Brown Book Group
100 Victoria Embankment
London EC4Y 0DY

An Hachette UK Company
www.hachette.co.uk

www.piatkus.co.uk

For my husband Mike
(to whom else could I possibly
dedicate a female survival guide!)

About the Author

Jo Haigh trained as a lawyer at the University of Leeds but changed direction early on, ultimately becoming finance director and company secretary of a public company subsidiary food group. Here she was involved in both a management buy-out and disposal to a public company, as well as several acquisitions.

On having children, she rather misguidedly believed that running her own business would give her more time, and she established a multidisciplinary consultancy which she owned for nearly ten years, holding numerous non-executive director roles. At the same time she developed a national reputation as a public speaker on corporate governance and mergers and acquisitions with the Institute of Directors and similar organisations.

Jo Haigh is head of corporate finance at MMG, a firm of specialist advisers based in London and Yorkshire. When relaxing (which isn't very often) she likes to travel and visit her homes in Deauville and Estapona, where her husband hides her phone and BlackBerry – but she always finds them!

Contents

Acknowledgements   viii

List of Contributors   ix

Introduction   1

Chapter 1   Getting Past Go   9

Chapter 2   Keeping the Hatchets from Your Head   45

Chapter 3   Work/Life Balance: Fact or Fiction?   57

Chapter 4   Office Couture – Make it Work for You   87

Chapter 5   Playing Games   103

Chapter 6   Education, Education, Education   125

Chapter 7   Getting Noticed   141

Chapter 8   Lies, Damned Lies and Politics!   157

Chapter 9   ♀   173

Chapter 10   Do a Frank Sinatra   187

Resources   219

Index   231

Acknowledgements

To my lovely publisher Piatkus for giving me the opportunity to write this book, which was certainly out of my comfort zone! And for Albert DePetrillo for believing I could write it.

To Caroline and Natalie whose wonderful help deciphering my awful handwriting is invaluable – ladies, you are absolutely fantastic, there would not be a book without your help and good humour.

To wonderful women out there everywhere: young, old, workaholics, entrepreneurs, movers, shakers, mothers, wives, partners, an all-round fabulous species. Without you there would be no book and no audience. I have loved interviewing every last one of you and learned so much on the way. My heartfelt thanks.

Special thanks to Denise Dwyer and Karen Farrington for their fantastic guidance and support.

And last but certainly not least, to my wonderful special girlfriends (you know who you are!), you have and always will make me complete.

List of Contributors

Deborah Adshead, joint MD of JD Approach

Pooya Ahmadi, CEO of the Business Channel

Sonita Alleyne, CEO of Somethin' Else

Kate Ancketill, MD and sole shareholder of GDR Creative Intelligence

Clare Balding, sports presenter at the BBC

Victoria Bannister, MD of Sportsshoes Unlimited

Christine Booth, Executive Dean, Faculty of Organisation and Management, Sheffield Hallam University

Deirdre Bounds, CEO of i-to-i

Alison Boxall, MD of Izziwizzikids

Anita Brough, sales and marketing director of Russell Richardson & Sons Limited

Sandra Brown OBE, founder of the Moira Anderson Foundation

Gail Carter, owner of Business Support Services

Sue Catling, parliamentary candidate for the Conservative Party

Alexis Cleveland, director general for Transformational Government and head of Cabinet Office Management

Denise Collins, group HR director of 3i

Rosemary Conley, TV personality

Lesley Cowley, CEO of Nominet UK

Fiona Cruickshank, managing director of the Specials Laboratory Limited

Sarah Deaves, chief executive of Coutts & Co

Justine Dignam, group marketing director of the Media Management Group (MMG)

Jayne Doherty, MD of Joyce Estate Agents

Natalie Douglas, CEO of IDIS Limited

Wendy Duckham, sales and marketing director of Construction Speciality UK Limited

Laurianne Enos, sole proprietor of Laurianne

Hannah Evans, founder of Piccalilly

Rolline Frewen, MD of The Admirable Crichton

Julia Gash, founder and director of Gash UK Limited

Diana Green, Vice Chancellor of Sheffield Hallam University

Dr Jane Guise, CEO of the Royal Bath & West of England Society

Barbara Harvey, Assistant Dean, Faculty of Organisation and Management, Sheffield Hallam University

Lynda Hinxman, Assistant Dean at Sheffield Hallam University

Angela Hughes, commercial director of JVL Products Limited

Nicola Kay, CEO, MD and major shareholder of Camden Electronics Limited

Alison Kennedy, programme manager and trainer at Salford University and 4C Change Limited

Julie Kenny CBE , MD and founder shareholder of Pyronix Limited

Joy Kingsley, MD of Pannone LLP

Pinky Lilani, founder of Spice Magic Limited

Anne Lockwood, MD of First Choice Select Limited

Yvonne Lumley, company director of Leading Women/People Factors

Heather MacDonald, principal and chief executive of Wakefield College

Helen Merfield, CEO of Health and Case Management Limited

Julia Moir, CEO of London Calling

Nicole Paradise, managing partner of Nabarro

Nicky Pattinson, MD of Hiya, It's Nicky

Jeanette Sargent, owner/director of Jeanette Sargent Limited

Barbara Scandrett, MD of Complete Case Management Limited

Dianne Sharp, MD of Mechetronics Limited

Fay Sharpe, director and shareholder of Zibrant

Fiona Sheridan, business risk partner in Risk Advisory Services at Ernst & Young

Ruth Spellman, CEO of Institute of Mechanical Engineers

Fiona Vanstone, PA to chairman and manager of head office, AMEC plc

Christina Vaughan, CEO and founder of Image Source Limited

Tracy Viner, owner and MD of Tracy Viner Limited

Perween Warsi, founder and chief executive of S&A Foods

Ann Worrall, MD of Stokvis Tapes

Remember, women in business are the future.
A softer approach does not mean a weak one.
Julia Moir, author

Introduction

Nobody can make you feel inferior without your permission.
Eleanor Roosevelt

If you put a small value on yourself, rest assured that the world will not raise your price.
Anon

What are your top tips for creating a successful enterprise? (Part 1)

Believe in yourself. **Rolline Frewen**

Make it happen rather than waiting for it to happen. Don't dwell on negatives. **Laurianne Enos**

I haven't a clue how I got here but it all seems to work. I have high expectations of everyone and my staff want to work in a successful business. **Christine Booth**

Deal fairly and firmly with those who can't perform. **Joy Kingsley**

Nine times out of ten you can find solutions to problems. You need to be creative in your problem solving and be prepared to learn. **Julie Kenny**

Be focused on your goals. **Denise Collins**

Get a mentor. **Gail Carter**

Focus, creativity, innovation and integrity. Never, ever give up. **Christina Vaughan**

Know where you are going. **Jayne Doherty**

Be clear about your mission and principles. Find a suitable narrative and repeat it, repeat it, repeat it. **Alexis Cleveland**

Give people confidence, be outward looking and be receptive to ideas. Harness passion, innovation and creativity. **Barbara Harvey**

In scaling the greasy pole that leads to the boardroom table most women will have been told at some point they are not equal to the task. It is likely they will have overcome overt or unexpressed scepticism on the grounds of gender rather than performance. If they have not had to overcome someone's lack of faith in them they will almost certainly have had to do battle with inner demons and the devil of self-doubt. Many women feel they need to change their personality and ignore their inherent nurturing qualities to get to the top in the business world.

At home they may have a husband, children, ageing parents, wayward siblings, all needy and reliant. Every day they must wrestle with the burden of knowledge that an oversight at work will cost the company dear, a slip-up at home will bring family life to a grinding halt.

This may be a bleak view of life for women in executive positions, but it's a view shared by some of this country's most significant businesswomen. The evidence is piled right here on my desk, in the form of interviews that tell a remarkable story of womanhood.

A plethora of books exist covering almost every conceivable angle of professional and corporate development. Some of these are tailored for the female entrepreneur or professional, but most have an androgynous feel. I believe women can and do succeed in business without sacrificing their inherent female qualities. This book is for those women who find themselves in a largely male-dominated field or anticipate they might be at some point. Those occupations are diverse and include not just finance, accountancy and legal organisations, but sport, recruitment, politics and many more. I have tried to give inspiration, explanation and frustration-busting techniques to help swell the numbers of us occupying high-level executive roles.

It's been a long haul for women to work their way out of the kitchen or the typing pool into the upper echelons of management. My own mother was a sheet metal engineer, a surprising career for a woman but even more extraordinary in the 1960s and 70s. When I was a teenager she told me she sincerely believed it would be better and easier for me to be able to pursue my career of choice when it was my turn to work, and those words 'better' and 'easier' have stayed in my mind for many years.

Are things better now than they were forty years ago? Well, my mother was a woman alone in a man's world and although the modern workplace is far from balanced, a solitary woman in an industry is rare today. So if increased job availability means better, then certainly her prediction has come true. If better implies more legally enforceable rights, well, that checks out too. During my working life, a considerable amount of legislation has been developed to aid and protect the female professional.

But easier – I am not so sure. In many ways I think it has become harder for women to succeed in their career of choice. Just because we have been offered more opportunities doesn't mean we are able, or even desire, to seize the chances in the workplace given the multitude of other tasks women have to do at any one time. Many of us, for different reasons, are squashed against the glass ceiling, mustard keen and meticulous but mired down, conscientious but constrained, ambitious yet still operating with one arm tied behind our backs.

Although the playing field isn't always level there are more women taking top jobs than ever before. Their success tells us that some important battles are being won and will, I trust, be a beacon for other women as they become increasingly accomplished in the executive arena.

There is often a perceived belief that all successful women are super-confident, able and impossibly determined. Very often this couldn't be further from the truth. It's just that many of us are incredibly good actresses and indeed no one, least of all me, would deny that the ability to act is an immensely important skill. That's because a confident veneer usually brings about a polished performance, and one skilfully managed performance usually leads to another. As an observer, don't be worried by it. Be inspired. Skills like these can be learned if they are not inherent.

If I attribute anything to my success, it would have to be an insatiable desire to excel and achieve a goal attached to a constantly moving target. And certainly, women are excelling in many areas. They continue to embrace further education. In 2000, 53 per cent of all degree applications came from women, although unfortunately not always in those subjects that can achieve top salaries, such as IT and engineering, but it's a start. With increasing legislation to protect against discrimination, female executives are on the increase, 180 per cent in the last ten years making a total of over 22 per cent of all executives female.

Although there are not nearly a representative number of women in FTSE 100 companies, it is worthwhile mentioning that 72 per cent of the companies in the top fifty have female directors, compared with 44 per cent of those in the bottom fifty. Slip over the water to our American cousins, and 84 per cent of the top 500 companies have women on their boards. Unfortunately the UK still has an unhealthy desire to attract to their boards white, middle-class, middle-aged men from similar school and university backgrounds. This male stereotyping creates an exclusion zone for many women who simply don't and never will fit into this old boys' club.

We often exclude ourselves from many opportunities by avoiding vital after-hours socialising, either from a lack of desire, or more often from a lack of time due to family pressures. In my experience, women are often reticent about being seen to be overtly ambitious. Many of our male colleagues have no such qualms and are first in the queue when putting a hand up for an opportunity.

On the positive side, many men recognise that they are more than capable of supporting the female wage earner. Office of National Statistics records show more than 100 per cent increase in house husbands in the last five years from 44,000 to 99,000. As any career woman will tell you, you need support at home, so maybe this is a start.

However, we still have a long way to go. For instance:

- only 5 per cent of all directors in the UK's FTSE 100 companies are female

- of those companies, 45 per cent have exclusively male boards

- only 12 per cent of non-executive roles in FTSE 100 companies are held by women.

Even if you do reach such high echelons, don't expect to be paid the same. By and large, a full-time female worker earns 82 per cent of their male colleagues' salary, and if she is part-time, only 60 per cent. For an averagely qualified woman, that is effectively a gap in earnings of over £250,000 in a lifetime's work. Even within a standard managerial job, a woman may often expect to earn £30,000 less than a man in the same position. In 2006 the *Guardian* revealed a list of 105 top businesses with directors earning over £1 million (amounting to 187 individuals); there was not one woman on the list. Sympathy may wane for the super-rich businesswomen who can afford to miss out on a few million without feeling the pinch but it would appear that the pay gap exists across the board, no matter whether you are a substantial earner or a modest one. Interestingly, the gender-salary gap is less visible elsewhere in Europe, particularly in France or Germany where male and female salaries are more on a par.

As far as maternity leave is concerned, Britain is certainly one of the least attractive places to work, particularly compared to Italy where you get five months paid leave, or Finland where you get nine!

The women I have interviewed, the great, the good and the under-recognised, have provided a wonderful and first-hand insight into corporate existence. They come from many different backgrounds, and are not only surviving but thriving. They are incisive and inspirational, and talking to them made me feel proud to be part of the fairer sex. These are women who experience real problems day in, day out. In many cases they have faced astonishingly difficult business circumstances and have come through to the other side, proving the saying that 'what doesn't kill you will make you stronger'.

Please share this book with your daughter, niece, granddaughter or any female relation or friend. As a mother of three daughters (two of mine and one on permanent loan), all ambitious, able and naturally beautiful, I hope they may read and learn from my mistakes and those of my many wonderful contributors.

Before writing the book I questioned whether the glass ceiling – that invisible shield that stops women progressing in business – really existed. By the end I was in no doubt that it does, even in this enlightened age. Sometimes the glass ceiling is put there by bosses or colleagues, determined that women shall not pass. But the pressure being applied by women everywhere makes me confident it will soon be shattered. It will no longer be a case of tales from the glass ceiling, rather a view from the top.

CHAPTER 1

Getting Past Go

Whatever women do they must do twice as well as men to be thought half as good. Luckily, this is not difficult.
Charlotte Whitton, author

What is the most memorable hurdle you have encountered?

People who were afraid of change. **Ruth Spellman**

That other people didn't share my self-belief. **Wendy Duckham**

Moving premises during a recession with two children at home. I was also doing a part-time job just to survive. **Ann Worrall**

People's perceptions that I was too young and inexperienced to be running an international business. I focused on my vision and an inner belief that I would succeed. **Christina Vaughan**

A lack of confidence. **Alison Kennedy**

A shortage of self-belief and excess of self-doubt. **Yvonne Lumley**

Changing roles from a company I built myself to a traditional business run by ex-forces people. **Dr Jane Guise**

Public speaking. I used to be terrified so I practised by volunteering and then began to enjoy it. **Pinky Lilani**

Achieving in junior and middle management roles isn't a problem for the professional female manager. It's the high road into the boardroom or on to top executive teams that seems to be strewn with apparently insurmountable obstacles.

I'll begin with my story, a swift track-back through my life revealing how I cleared some of the hurdles that lay in my path. I was disappointed but not surprised to find chauvinism rearing its head early in my career. (I'm concerned and outraged that it still exists.) However, I was floored by the immense responsibilities that came to my door in the wake of success and directorships. Understanding how I could soon author my own downfall by a slip of the tongue or an ill-placed comment was also a shock to the system. Looking back, I realise I have learned as much about myself as any of the businesses I have been in.

This chapter describes barriers that may lie in the path of today's aspiring businesswomen as they try to scale the fortresses built by men at work. It will also provide advice and real examples of how the walls of the executive citadel can be knocked down or navigated to help lever women into the boardroom.

My Story

1957   Born in back-to-back house in small Yorkshire village
1968   Failed the eleven-plus
1972   Went to the local technical college

1975	Acquired three A grades at A level and went to Leeds University to study law
1978	Took my first job in industry for funeral wreath manufacturers and studied for professional exams as company secretary Moved and advanced several times
1983	Became financial controller and company secretary of major food and wine importers and chain of restaurants
1985	First directorship of a £30 million acquisitive business
1986	First daughter, Jessica, is born
1987	The business I work for is sold with my help to a major public company and I am made group finance director and company secretary
1989	Second daughter, Pollyanna, is born Start my own company from the back bedroom During this period I hold approximately thirty different non-executive directorships across a large array of businesses
1991	Divorced
1994	Remarried
2000	Sold my business to my management team
2001	Joined national accountancy practice to establish regional corporate finance provision
2008	Moved on to pastures new with London specialist media management company as head of corporate finance

My very first job after leaving university was as trainee book-keeper and wages clerk, while I studied for my first professional exam. My wage in 1979 was £40 per week, in today's terms probably about £150 a week. Straight out of university and living at home, this was more money than I'd ever had. This wasn't disposable income, it was just income! In those days I was paid weekly and in cash, and the sight and smell of those one-pound notes is still a vivid memory.

I worked at a wire-processing company that, of all things, made funeral wreaths; not glamorous, certainly not very clean and definitely not at all female orientated. Boredom soon set in. The trouble with a university education, at least in the 1970s, was that you emerged from the system with the absolute certainty you would be snapped up by blue-chip employers.

In fact, I joined this firm because it had offered to fund my professional training and I was fed up with having no money. I could, of course, have gone with a professional practice but the wages were even lower and I had reckoned on the fact that a qualification achieved in industry would ultimately offer more. If I'd had a vision of a rapid rise to the exalted heights of the boardroom, I was soon to experience a harsh reality check.

Even the office junior knew more than I did and was certainly held in higher esteem, particularly when it became painfully evident that I knew very little, not even the difference between an invoice and a statement. I certainly never thought it would be my job to file such things.

My degree had awarded me such arrogance that I felt by simply stuffing all the records I was dealing with in one hanging file they would leave my desk for ever and would become somebody else's problem. Thankfully – and I really mean that – Christine, the fearsome office manager, brought me right down to earth with a bump. I came in one morning to find the entire contents of the filing cupboard in a pile by my desk, with a note saying sort it out – or else. Being made accountable for some of the less appetising sides of business at such an early stage in my career was probably one of the best things that could have happened.

Providentially, opportunities presented themselves in short order and I worked hard to take advantage of them. By the age of twenty-four I had my qualification and had learned a lot with a rapidly growing and ambitious business as their management accountant.

Often successful people need some kind of a mentor. The concept of mentoring is the provision of one-to-one personal support and encouragement from a more accomplished business person to one with less experience. If you are fortunate enough to have a mentor then you have someone you can talk to about business or indeed other issues, who will encourage and guide you through various stages of your career by drawing on their own seasoned wisdom. I was lucky in that I found mine by accident in the shape of my then managing director, who perhaps recognised and rewarded the drive and ambition within me but above all gave me opportunities and reassurance which helped me develop. If you strike up a successful mentoring arrangement that gives you room to grow, then you are indeed blessed. If you don't have a mentor, find one. It doesn't have to be someone inside your organisation but, as we all have various crises of confidence, at some time early in your career you will need someone to nurture and support you.

Fate plays its cards at random, some fall in your favour, some do not. Fate dealt me an opportunist's hand when one of my employer's former directors died suddenly and tragically. Mutation and transformation often come in the wake of disaster and on this occasion my managing director and mentor decided to carry out a management buyout. I was to be an important figure in the process.

The opportunity, although rooted on such unfortunate footings, meant that at the ripe old age of twenty-six I was offered rapid promotion to financial controller of what was to become a £30-million-plus organisation. The business was expanding at an incredible pace and five years out of university I was now managing a four-strong team, all of them much older than me, and two of them men. This was tricky, as my management skills were raw to put it mildly. But my mentor, to whom I owe so much, kept the faith by coaching and supporting me.

Three years later the business took a further quantum leap as it diversified into other areas and at age twenty-nine I was offered my first directorship. Now, I was finance director of a group of companies by then turning over some £45 million plus, not a small business by today's standards and certainly not in the mid-1980s.

Still, my own propulsion up the company ladder had been very protected. I had been sustained and cared for, thanks to the mentoring process, and I was wholly prepared for the experience of being part of the board, but before I had got used to the idea, the company changed yet again. Within one year of my appointment the shareholders were approached to sell the business to an investment company. The offer was simply too attractive to dismiss and my role and responsibilities were to change irreversibly.

Although our business was substantial, it was nothing compared to our new big brother. We were minnows and not particularly slick ones at that.

The investment company owned several organisations, many of them different from our own. Being a director of a subsidiary of a public company as opposed to being a director of an owner-managed business could not have been more different. Some of these critical differences included not just the way we reported our information, both technical and management, but how we looked. Suddenly we had to ask a credit committee if we wanted to spend. Our budget was torn apart and our strategy criticised by third parties. We had to change from long-standing and much-loved local professional advisers and banks to cold-faced strangers. All very scary.

In retrospect the biggest actual differences were much more subtle as reporting lines were changed. Instead of reporting to my MD, I now found myself reporting to the group finance director. A man, of course, and a terrifying one at that. I had to join the other subsidiary finance directors on a monthly basis to justify our results or, worse still, to answer for failures in the forecast performance. The pressure was much more intense. After all, we had tens of thousands of shareholders to answer to, so I guess it wasn't surprising.

Decisions took for ever to make. I had been used to working in a small company in which we made a lot of the decisions on the hoof. No more. Everything needed approval from on high and, if you didn't get it, God help you. It was a massive learning curve.

Responsibilities of a Director

So you want to be a company director or even own the business you are in. The power, the prestige, the creative freedom and the extra cash all sound alluring. But do you really know what you are letting yourself in for as you stick a flag in the summit of your ambition? Your responsibilities as a director are certainly substantial. As you can see from the partial list below, you need to depend not only on your own skills but on those of the people around you to keep on the right side of the law. When I took up my first directorship I had absolutely no idea of the scope of my liabilities. You may not even want such onerous liabilities, when you discover their extent (see another of my books *The Business Rules* for more information).

Here are some examples to give you food for thought:

■ Personal liability for unpaid creditors if you trade when your company is insolvent.

■ Personal liability for the health and safety of staff – and even intruders – which, if breached, can result in prison sentences.

■ Financial liability, both personal and corporate, for late filing of accounts and other statutory information.

■ A duty to consider the impact of your company's actions on the environment.

■ A list a mile long of obligations under employment law, including the requirement to consult with your staff on critical issues that affect their well-being.

■ Personal liabilities for non-performance in relation to contracts you have guaranteed, including banking agreements.

■ The requirement to ensure that the company maintains proper records consistent with any report from auditors.

■ And on and on . . . and on.

Indeed, if most people had any real idea of their liabilities in this arena they would never leave the comfort of their sitting rooms.

Assuming, however, you accept this is part of the package, your success and performance are what should keep you in post and see you moving onward and upward. (I say 'should' because naturally sometimes even the best people become part of corporate casualties through no fault of their own. As these are areas you can't control I prefer to concentrate on those areas you *can* manage.)

SWOT

Men are taught to apologise for their weaknesses,
women for their strengths.
Lois Wyse, author

If getting to the board is one thing, trust me, staying there, particularly in companies with ambitious boards and management teams, is another. Men as well as women are likely to be stabbed in the back. Your best form of defence to stay in your post is your ability to deliver consistently and well.

No one is perfect but you are likely to be judged not only on your positive attributes or strengths but on your negative attributes or weaknesses and particularly so if you are the token woman. Often managers and directors undertake SWOT analysis. This stands for Strength, Weakness, Opportunities and Threats. The aim is to capitalise on the first, eliminate the second, seize on the third and counter the fourth. But that's the simplistic approach because strengths can also be weaknesses and vice versa.

With or without SWOT input, my first tip is to acknowledge your own strengths and weaknesses. If you don't think you can clearly identify these ask a good friend or your partner. This is a painful process so add an extra layer of skin before you start.

My best friend Angela tells me I am positively anal in my obsession for order. I know this makes me a poor delegator and annoys the hell out of colleagues. On the other hand it means that big muddles are rare because my approach is so thorough. My husband tells me I have a short fuse. That's clearly negative but from a positive point of view (I am struggling here) everyone is absolutely clear about what is expected.

Experience tells me men are more forgiving than women and less likely to bear a grudge. Women are less charitable, particularly if they have been on the receiving end of any unacceptable behaviour. Like elephants they tend never to forget. If you sit on a board with other women, you may need a more refined approach, whereas my experience with male board colleagues is that subtlety is usually lost on them.

My anally retentive qualities have meant that I am particularly prescriptive with regards to the meeting of deadlines. As far as I am concerned, a deadline is just that – immovable. Only the four horsemen of the apocalypse could make me change. Most of the female board directors I have worked with are the same. For male colleagues, however, a deadline is often something one may like to aspire to achieve, but on the whole can be moved. I have never found this characteristic of mine a particular obstacle in getting on a board, but I will admit it has on occasions rendered me the school swot and has given me another black mark in my popularity contest. Maybe not with my MD or chairman, but certainly with my director peers.

BOARDROOM SURVIVAL GUIDE

I had to learn survival techniques quickly to cope on the board, many of which were to hold me in good stead in the years to come. Here are a few:

■ Introduce yourself first. Give your title and then your name.

■ Sit as near to the chairman or head of the table as possible.

- Ask questions and offer opinions but don't talk over people.

- If you don't understand something, don't be afraid to ask for clarification. The chances are, if you don't understand neither will other people, but they possibly aren't sufficiently confident to admit their lack of knowledge.

- Prepare in advance for meetings but avoid looking like a clever clogs.

- Never belittle anyone in a meeting – even if someone does this to you. You will gain more respect by dealing with such matters in private.

- If a colleague blatantly plagiarises your ideas in a meeting, make sure you deal with this at the proper time and in the appropriate way – but do deal with it. Likewise always give acknowledgement for other people's ideas.

- Speak coherently and firmly, don't whisper, be coy or fumble. Don't shout and especially don't cry. Colleagues don't know how to deal with this. If you feel you are losing control ask for a break and get a cup of tea and some air. If you are near to tears, it's important not to look downward because that brings them on more quickly.

- Take your own dated notes – which amounts to keeping a business record diary.

■ Be prepared to stand down or compromise if you believe your case is no longer valid. Digging your heels in for the sake of it never takes you forward. Being stubborn is, generally speaking, a male trait so leave it to the experts. Try to rise above rather than burrow down below.

■ Don't be bullied. I was teased and bullied mercilessly and I learned the only way to deal with this was by not rising to the bait. Eventually, as all bullies do, they got bored and left me alone.

■ Retain a sense of humour. I am far too serious for my own benefit. It's a definite failing I've recognised in myself. Learn to laugh with others and, most importantly, at yourself.

■ Don't accept second best. On the other hand, compromise may be needed. Learn the essentials of give and take so you can confidently decide which path is most appropriate.

Discrimination

I ask no favours for my sex . . . All I ask of our brethren is that they will take their feet from off our necks.
Sarah Moore Grimké, abolitionist and suffragist

In a perfect world, people would not be judged on gender but on ability. However, the world is flawed as are most of the people in it.

That includes many male inhabitants of the boardroom who, histori-cally, have been responsible for helping to keep women out of the executive loop. It is human failing that keeps women down, and a commercial catastrophe that it still happens. Some examples of discrimination I've encountered either through experience or contact with other women are nothing short of outrageous.

When I became pregnant with my second child, it was well before today's more enlightened maternity laws. I recall I was asked: 'So I suppose we won't see you after 3.30 p.m. each day?' Of course, these comments are all but outlawed now. But at the time questions like that induced an overwhelming level of guilt. In those days the culture of success was linked to being first in the office in the morning and last out at night. In hindsight, I probably missed out on a tremendous amount of time with both my daughters because I felt duty bound to be in the office.

I was the only woman director in the whole company. The comfort-able (but entirely professional) approach we once had to meetings as well as general decision making had changed beyond recognition. My unique position as the token female was regarded with scepticism at best and with downright ignorance at worst. Some things have clearly changed (well, I hope they have) but I can't count the number of times I was either completely ignored at board meetings, cut across or asked to make and pour the coffee and, of course, clear away the cups.

At one point in my career, I took on a temporary interim direc-torship of a well-known Yorkshire worsted manufacturer. The job, a board position, was to carry out a specific project that needed the support of the whole board if it was to be successful. On my first day the chief financial officer, a dinosaur left over from a previous age, told me that perhaps the other directors (all men, of course) and I would feel more comfortable if I didn't join them in the director's dining room. Impossible to believe he actually articulated those words. Even more baffling is the fact that I complied. Clearly I would take another route today because maturity brings with it an enhanced level of confidence, but I simply didn't have that kind of resilience in my armoury in those days.

This whole experience was a tough one. As the only female in a very male-dominated old-fashioned business, I recall having a meeting with the MD when he ordered a cup of tea for himself from his secretary and didn't even think to ask if I would like one. He then sat through the rest of the meeting sipping tea from a china cup and munching on his biscuit while I was dry-mouthed with rage. I was too shy at the time to say anything but it's a memory that will stay with me for ever. I thought this brand of rudeness and ignorance had being consigned to history – but some of my interviewees told a different story.

Polly Courtney, Analyst, City Investment Bank

I was the only woman in a team of twenty-one and this made a difference: I was seen as a secretary, not as a banker. When directors scanned the office for an analyst, I just didn't seem to be on their radar.

I was used to male-dominated environments. I'd been to an all-boys secondary school and had worked in engineering. I'd always given as good as I'd got but it was hard not to take personally comments such as 'When does your work experience end?', 'You must have slept your way into university' or 'Sorry, Polly, we would invite you along, but we're planning to pull tonight.' I was even told by colleagues that the only reason I got the job was because of my legs. It was a delicate balance, trying to prove my worth without over-proving it. There are lots of fragile egos in the City, so being too bold can do you more harm than good. Seeing my friends at Christmas was what finalised my decision to leave. They reminded me that there was more to life. (*Observer*, 27 August 2006)

It would be nice to imagine that Polly's experiences were isolated. But that doesn't seem to be true if the rash of sexism in the City discrimination cases seen already this century is anything to go by.

Although an average intake in a City firm may be split between the sexes, only 3 per cent of executives at the highest level are women. According to the Equal Opportunities Commission, women working full-time in banking and finance currently earn 55 per cent of their male counterparts' earnings.

Discrimination that's jaw-droppingly blatant is relatively easy to deal with. The Equal Pay Act of 1970 and the Sexual Discrimination Act of 1975 have at least put some punch into an unfair fight. But it is an underground movement of discrimination that's altogether harder to gauge. 'It is about the subtle discounting of ability,' Helena Dennison, chair of the City Women's Network, told the *Guardian* on 19 March 2001. 'Covert discrimination means rubbishing a woman's contribution during meetings, either with snide remarks or remarks about her appearance. Covert discrimination undermines confidence.' Dennison believes many woman don't take their grievances to court for fear of gaining reputations as troublemakers. 'If you were making £300,000 a year, would you jeopardise your career by speaking out against the firm?'

'Sexism is more dangerous now,' Justine Burgess, who used to work in international equity, says in the same article. When her boss pulled her on to his knee or massaged her shoulders when she was on the phone to a client, she found the situation relatively easy to diffuse. 'I could laugh it off,' she says. 'What is more difficult is an environment in which you get fewer daily comments, but a lot of subtle discrimination over promotions and pay.' One of her friends filed a suit against a merchant bank after being passed over for promotion because, she suspects, she couldn't play golf. 'She was out of that whole guy thing and although she brought in as much revenue as the rest of them, they froze her out.'

How do you deal with discrimination in the workplace?

Jayne Doherty says you should 'Recognise it won't be easy. Blokes generally won't give you respect. One guy told me he would get me thrown off the project if I didn't sleep with him. My then manager just laughed at me when I told him. Be strong and know your own mind.'

Kate Ancketill refuses to be thrown off balance by the quiet sexism that she once encountered regularly. 'People always assumed I was the secretary even when I was the MD. I have always been hands on, working closely alongside with my staff. I filed that stuff away. Personally, I like people who are nice to everyone, powerful or not. I remembered the people who did that and now I might choose not to spend my time with them although I wouldn't let my feelings affect a professional relationship.'

Clare Balding, a sports presenter with the BBC, was incensed with the reception she received from event organisers when she went to a darts tournament. 'I was seething underneath but didn't show it. I try to prove people like that wrong by being the best I can be.'

My investigations among fellow female entrepreneurs reveal sexism has been widespread in the recent past. So if it's no longer the astonishing up-front and shameless variety, how do you spot sexism at work today? Here's a quick guide to what may be going on.

- Watch out for men who make less eye contact with women than they do with male colleagues.

- Some men frown when they speak to women, imparting negativity.

- Other men praise women workers more highly for their physical appearance than for their intellectual ability.

- These same men will respond to male colleagues with fulsome comment and constructive criticism – and to women with a non-committal 'uh-huh'.

- There are those who are quick to credit men with succesful ideas but neglect to mention who is responsible when the winning formula is authored by a woman.

- Men of this ilk are more likely to give men but not women detailed instructions for a task, and offer women less feedback, support or praise.

- Watch out for men who socialise only with other men during office or networking events.

■ Sometimes sexism is entirely unconscious, like the provision of
    an assistant for a man while a woman working in the same role
    is expected to manage their own administration.

Covert chauvinism was something Fiona Sheridan, business risk
partner in Risk Advisory Services at Ernst & Young, had to overcome
after moving from the Glasgow office of a prestigious accountancy
firm to head office in London.

> I didn't notice male domination too much in Scotland but in London
> it was very different. Meetings were arranged in pubs after work or
> on golf courses when I wasn't there. I work four days a week and have
> Fridays off. Sometimes meetings were arranged on a Friday inten-
> tionally so I couldn't attend. Now I will insist on rescheduling when
> I feel it's right.

Fiona Cruickshank, the managing director of a pharmaceutical
company, enjoyed cordial relations with her bank manager until
another partner joined the business she had started in 1999 at the
age of thirty-three. 'After that, the bank manager would only speak
to him even though he had happily dealt with me until then.' Fiona
took direct action to remedy the situation. She told the bank manager
in question why she was upset. He was so far behind the times he
hadn't even realised how he was behaving or the effect it was having.
Nonetheless, she changed banks at the earliest opportunity.

For Fiona Vanstone of AMEC plc the biggest issue she faced working
in construction was sexual harassment, although things improved
after she married. Her response to it was dignified. 'On the whole I
ignored it.'

But let's not lose sight of the good news. 'The workplace has changed so much in the last twenty years and it's all positive,' says Nicole Paradise, managing partner of Nabarro. 'I'm delighted to be a role model.'

Denise Collins, group HR director of 3i, on her experiences at Ford

I have not been bludgeoned to death by men. When I left university and joined Ford in industrial relations I had the time of my life, even though I was one of the few women there. It came down to me, tackling their prejudices rather than being a victim. It equipped me well for the future. I learned about multicultural environments and now nothing throws me off course.

DISCRIMINATION SURVIVAL GUIDE

Be objective about what's going on. Are you sure there's evidence of discrimination against you or are you being sucked in to office politics on a grand scale?

- Ignore it. Sometimes it's the best approach even if it smacks of defeatism. Not so long ago it was famously declared that life was too short to make a quiche. Well, sometimes its brief passage means that creating a fuss about sexism simply isn't worth the effort. I take this position with the benefit of years of experience behind me. I have agonised over comments made, not slept, cried and raged – and for what? Just a few more lines beneath my eyes. It's difficult to lobby for cultural change and achieve business success at the same time. Choose what's most important to you at the time.

■ That said, ignoring it is not always an option. It's undeniably important to question obvious injustices and sometimes that takes priority. After all, there should be a rota for answering the secretary's telephone when she is at lunch; it shouldn't always fall to one person, especially if that person is a woman on a par with men in the office.

■ Don't be shy about your skills and achievements. Send emails to relevant bosses if you have pulled off a commercial coup. Keeping quiet until someone notices is a risky policy to pursue.

■ Don't be negative about things you perceive as weaknesses. Flexible working hours and a family are not weaknesses so don't apologise for them.

■ Be sure you know how much you are worth. Women are notori-ous for undervaluing themselves. Be prepared to negotiate for higher wages and do it in a positive way, avoiding comparisons with colleagues. After all, you may have been misinformed about how much they earn.

■ Don't get mad, get even. You may have to wait for the right moment but usually the opportunity for revenge comes along eventually, preferably when your emotions have returned to an even keel. Don't be afraid to take your chances. If I am honest, this has been one of my critical career drivers.

■ Question how much you want the job. Don't be afraid to look elsewhere for work if your confidence is being seriously eroded or your life is being made miserable by sexism.

■ Use peer support. It's good to talk, especially for women, and the process of informally sharing information in cases that involve sexism can provide a necessary valve in a high-pressure situation.

■ Only fight battles you can win. Systemic sexism will be hard to overturn, no matter how righteous the cause.

■ Talk informally with your boss if you suspect sexism is playing a part in the office. Offer solutions rather than endless complaints.

■ Take expert advice. It may cost plenty of money but it's better to make an informed decision than a stab in the dark.

■ Remember, the path to an employment tribunal is a long one. Even if you start on the process it doesn't mean it has to end up in a legal battle. The first move could be a catalyst for change.

■ Consult the equal opportunities commission for advice.

■ Learn your lessons well. Become a pioneer against discrimination in your own corporate practices and, when you become a boss, stamp it out. As soon as it is possible for you to do so, create an office atmosphere where discrimination of any kind is utterly unacceptable.

The Popularity Contest

The thing women have yet to learn is nobody gives you power.
You just take it.
Roseanne Barr, actress

Coming through the management ranks I had generally been able to chase with the hounds and run with the proverbial hares. Not always, but often this helped me deal with my potent inner desire to be popular – to an extent a female failing and one I had been loath to acknowledge. But once you move into the boardroom, the blurred lines of 'them and us', sometimes appropriate in management roles particularly in smaller businesses, are so much more clearly defined.

I won't deny it was a very difficult transition period and my quest to be liked was undoubtedly an obstacle I had to overcome; although honestly I am not sure I ever really have. I still find it very difficult to be contentious. I want to be liked, particularly by colleagues and especially by my peers. It doesn't always pan out that way.

Most men I have dealt with in the boardroom by and large seem less concerned about this. That's not to say they don't want to be popular but only a few I have come across would let fears about lack of popularity stand in the way of their success.

Although this chapter promises ways of knocking down such obstacles, I generally prefer circumnavigation. I have chosen to separate my personal life from my business life (this initially does create other problems – see further chapters), getting the requisite support and friendship from my personal friends and family, especially my girlfriends, and continuing to try to accept that you cannot always be liked by everyone.

But if women like to be liked, men have a preference for power that leaves many women cold. Undermine those illusions of power at your peril. I found the boardroom to be much more of a battleground than the management stream, often full of immature and brittle egos. Many directors at all levels suffer some degree of insecurity. Some, particularly men, are better at hiding it, while many women I have encountered attempt to overcome it by overcompensating. Trouble is, it sounds like blowing your own trumpet and that's not a good way to sound.

My advice is to tread carefully round the 'Big I Am' trip, tempting as it may be to go there when others do. Strangely, the English still tend to favour failure and any overt success can attract derision at best and, at worst, ridicule. In simple words, as they say in Yorkshire, 'Don't lord it around.' There are other ways of getting recognition (see Chapter 7, Getting Noticed).

The Open Book

The reason there are so few female politicians is that it is too much trouble to put make-up on two faces.
Maureen Murphy, politician

If the boardroom can be a battleground at times, reputations, like wars, can be won and lost, often without too much engagement from the combatants. This applies to everyone but especially to women who tend to have more open dispositions – which can be detrimental to their success. One unguarded conversation may leave a women with her tender underbelly exposed to predators.

Still, the overall winner of the 'ill-chosen comment leading to disastrous consequences' award for the twentieth century goes to a man. Gerald Ratner is one of many people who was to discover that a few poorly judged words taken out of context can change the face of your career, though not always irretrievably. Ratner was at the head of a jewellery empire when he stood up to speak at the Institute of Directors in April 1991. The sherry decanter, glasses and silver-coloured tray sold in his stores were, he candidly admitted, 'total crap'. Further he spoke about earrings he sold for less than the price of a prawn sandwich that 'probably won't last as long'. After his words were reported across the next day's papers no less than £500 million was wiped off the value of the company. Within two years he was gone and in 1994 the name Ratner was erased from the company's outlets. Curiously, the day before the gaffe an analyst had asked him: 'What could go wrong?' He discovered to his cost that quite a bit could go wrong in an extremely short space of time.

Since then the term 'doing a Ratner' has been applied to anyone who criticises their products or disparages their customers. Perhaps it's a mark of the man that he continues to sell high-value jewellery successfully online.

As a director, not only do you have a perceived different level of authority to a manager but, scarily, an actual different level of authority. Your words could bind the company to contracts and obligations and even create a personal liability. A director has both an actual and a perceived right to make contracts. For example, the other party can insist on delivery or 'specific performance', i.e. the contract must be fulfilled. That means, for example, that if a director signs a cheque upon which the company's name is spelt incorrectly he, personally may, in certain circumstances, have to honour its payment. For example, if the company name on the chequebook says, 'Jo Haigh Limited', but the registered name at Companies House is 'Jo Haigh Ltd', then it is not a company cheque but a personal cheque, as the names have to be identical. Some people would like to think this makes no difference or that it's the banks responsibility – neither of which are true. Indemnity insurance offers a modicum of protection.

My own experience is that while men tend to play their cards close to their chest, women tend to take a more open approach. This can be something of an elephant trap. We sometimes have a tendency to say more than we should, sooner than we should. The consequences can be dire. In one role as full-time finance director whose job it was to report to the board on the monthly performance, I learned to be very wary indeed of giving away any premature indications of performance as I was inevitably wrong and, of course, was always held to blame.

My heartfelt advice? Think first, speak later. This can be surprisingly difficult for women who are dealing with a huge variety of activities at any one time. They gamely try to coordinate speed and volume of thought processes with speech pattern, frequently with disastrous results. Trust me, I speak from vast experience in this area.

Use the following rules to avoid a dash towards disaster:

- Take a deep breath before speaking so you do not rush to complete a sentence.

- Count to ten before jumping into a debate or conversation.

- Develop the art of instantly imagining how your words will sound to someone across the table with a different agenda to your own.

- Pour a glass of water or carry out a similarly mundane task while you wrestle with the words inside your head.

■ Recap on events so far or keep a few stock phrases that will trip off the tongue to buy you time before you speak. That means reeling off sentences that begin with 'On this occasion, in my opinion . . .' or 'Although at this point it might not seem this way to you, I can see that . . .' They may be short on meaning but they are useful devices in difficult situations.

Getting Past Go

So you've heard about all the hurdles I and others have had to face getting off the start mark. I've invited lots of eminent businesswomen to share with me stories of their 'first fence' and how they overcame it.

CASE STUDY

Nicky Pattinson, MD of Hiya, It's Nicky

Few have a story as compelling as Nicky Pattinson, who is now a successful speaker, writer, radio presenter and sales trainer. She shared her astonishing story with me in order to encourage women to go further along the executive path.

My mum and dad owned land in Holmfirth, where *Last of the Summer Wine* is filmed. I was brought up to believe I would inherit this land. That stopped me doing things I should have done. I also had a very broad Yorkshire accent. My mum always told me that, unless I improved the way I spoke and my demeanour, I would amount to very little. I almost bought into that and it did lower my self-esteem. But the one thing I could always do was hold a conversation. I never understood the power of that at the time. The penny didn't drop until much later.

At thirty she married and worked on a market stall with her husband, John, selling cakes and biscuits. Together they increased their turnover of £1,000 a week into an annual turnover of £1,500,000.

It wasn't just the stock that counted. Every market we operated had two or three stalls doing exactly the same; we were probably slightly more expensive than the others. But we found a way of selling so not only would people stand and queue but they would bring their friends. We made an emotional connection. We created a brand experience that was magnetic and engaging.

Soon she became pregnant with her son Jackson. 'I worked right up to having him, six days a week from six a.m. to seven in the evening, often crying with tiredness. But I was driven. I was looking for approval, for someone to say you are fantastic, I really appreciate what you are doing. Instead I had a husband who thought I was lazy.' Because Nicky continued working frantically, Jackson, her striking-looking firstborn went to nursery despite her premonitions of dread. It was here, aged four and a half months, that he was found dead after being put down for a sleep. Witnesses said he had been left to scream. Although the post-mortem failed to determine the cause, it was widely thought to be a cot death.

Nicky was told about Jackson's death in an emotionally charged telephone call.

That phone call changed my life. Things could never, ever be the same. You don't realise you have a heart until it is broken, or a soul until it is shattered into little pieces. Afterwards I wanted to break my arms and legs so I could feel the same intense pain somewhere else in my body.

As she packed up Jackson's belongings the day after his death she watched the weather forecaster on breakfast television. '"What *is* she on about?" I asked my husband. "Don't they know the world has ended?" There is utter terror – anyone who has lost a child will tell you that. You don't know how you can live the rest of your life without that person in it.'

Her son's death marked the start of a string of personal disasters: her mum died after going into hospital for routine surgery; the business began to fail alongside her marriage; her father was suffering from terminal cancer. The only bright spot was the birth of a second son Dhani. At her lowest ebb Nicky was living on income support, fending off creditors and watching her inheritance being eaten up in an acrimonious divorce settlement. What was left was taken by cowboy builders as she fruitlessly tried to repair her future. 'When you are dead in the road, the buzzards will find you,' she observed.

Eventually she got a job at a prestigious design agency. She was soon bringing in hundreds of thousands of pounds worth of business. 'All I did was take the lessons I had learned on the market and tweak them.' It's a formula she now passes on to others through her own business, multiplying their sales potential many fold.

Today, it is almost like I'm talking about somebody else. However, when I am standing in front of an audience of a thousand people, the raw emotions come back and I'm laid bare. The long-term effect of it is that I can stand a lot of things, I consider myself a tough person. Not very many things frighten me, but if I hear a baby screaming it brings up grief that comes from the solar plexus over which I have only limited control. Although I desperately miss the young man I would have been arguing with now about who empties the dishwasher, I'm grateful for the experience of losing him at four and a half months and for the time I had with him. That was his destiny, this is mine. I wouldn't have missed a single day.

CASE STUDY
Kate Ancketill, MD of GDR Creative Intelligence

Kate Ancketill's business was shaped by an entirely different tragedy. She began a company centring on trend analysis in retail and leisure in 2000. It was still only a fledgling when 9/11 occurred. In addition to the terrible toll in human life, the event catastrophically undermined the commercial world.

Retail trend analysis was seen by some clients as nice to have, but not essential. When economic foundations shake, it is almost impossible to get established in a business where you are not seen as essential, and the phone didn't ring for two years. Perhaps we weren't as good then as we are now but everybody was hunkering down, protecting limited budgets. Lots of people were laid off at the time.

Kate refused to contemplate redundancies in her small company so she took as little salary as possible for herself, paid for groceries with credit cards and sublet some of the office space.

We became lean and mean. The only way was up. Because I never had much when I was growing up, I didn't miss it when I didn't have it then. In fact, people need our services more in a downturn. Our problem at the time was that we were going in at the bottom, dealing with relatively junior people who didn't have the budget to use us. Now we see many more senior people who are aware that in tough times innovation is important.

Now her company, of which she is managing director and sole shareholder, has thirteen staff.

CASE STUDY

Rolline Frewen, MD of The Admirable Crichton

Rolline Frewen and her business partner, Johnny Roxburgh, run The Admirable Crichton, a catering and party-design firm that is best known for its big ideas. Once they built a marquee in ten sections between Edinburgh's Princes Street and the castle, creating a burn running through the middle over which was suspended a dance floor with cutaway sections revealing the fish swimming beneath. On another occasion at the Royal Academy they had actors dressed in a way that made them appear to be naked, a giant poodle made from pink carnations and mock flamingos lining the stairs. In 2005 the company catered the queen's celebration lunch for 2,000 war veterans at Buckingham Palace. The year before that it arranged two prestigious dinners for heads of state and senior sponsors at the Athens Olympics. 'Our minimum order is five thousand pounds and no one has yet spent two million pounds on a party with us,' Rolline remarked.

Business has snowballed since it began more than a quarter of a century ago and the bond with her business partner is strong. 'It wouldn't happen without the two of us. My strengths fill the gaps left by his weaknesses and vice versa.'

Rolline Frewen has been with her business partner much longer than she has been married to her husband. But it was her superior earning power rather than 'the other man' that threw up a problem casting a shadow over her marriage to her land-agent husband.

Any problems we had were perceived more than real. I hated the fact that I paid when we went out to a restaurant. He did too, but not nearly as much as me. I felt so uncomfortable because that wasn't what I was brought up to know. I felt as if I had my right foot in my left shoe. Finally it just had to be addressed. You have to discuss these things.

How did you overcome difficult hurdles?

REAL-TIME HURDLES

Sometimes the hurdles you face are the physical kind, easy to identify and the type that, with a bit of planning and a lot of luck, can be overcome.

Pooya Ahmadi sees herself as a creator and visionary. Nonetheless, when the future of the business depended on ready cash, she had to roll her sleeves up and get grafting. 'I had to raise three million pounds in a week. It was the hardest thing in the world yet in some ways the easiest thing to do as I was so focused.'

Anne Lockwood 'I was tendering for a large piece of business within our first few months of operation and we were up against all the big players in the market place. I recall pulling up in the car park in my humble Metro right outside the office where we were to do our presentation and parking between a Rolls-Royce (belonging to the company owner who had just done his presentation) and a BMW (belonging to someone on after us). Nerves were already running high when I discovered the panel numbered six. But we had prepared our presentation well, we had rehearsed it thoroughly and, although there were signs of nerves, it went well. I believe our passion for the industry and our eagerness to secure the contract came through and we won it on a year's trial. We are now in our fourteenth year of trading with that company.'

Victoria Bannister Some might envy Victoria Bannister her sports gear empire which was passed down to her from her father who started the company. She shadowed him for four years so there was a seamless transfer in the managing directorship. However, she remembers: 'It was a war of attrition at times getting the reins of power off my dad.'

INTANGIBLE HURDLES

Sometimes the barrier that's penning you in isn't so easy to identify and only a chunk of self-knowledge coupled with determination can get you over the top into better territory.

Lesley Cowley For Lesley it was going back to work after the birth of her son. 'I realised I needed support from friends and family and had to ignore the people who so obviously disapproved of what I was doing.'

Jeanette Sargent was gripped by fear when she handed her notice in, kissing goodbye to a monthly salary and the related perks. 'I overcame my issues about losing regular money by constantly reading start-up business and entrepreneur books and coached myself to stop focusing on the lack of it, concentrating instead on my future success.'

INNER HURDLES

For many women the answers lie within their own hands. The barriers thrown up come from within – and are no less powerful for that. Often, age and experience provide the solutions they seek.

Anon An anonymous contributor remembers how a lack of confidence in her own abilities stopped her voicing a contradictory opinion. Her assumption was that others round the table knew more than she did. She remedied the problem by taking a degree as a physical proof of her inner resources.

Tracy Viner was also hampered by confidence and self-belief issues. 'I always used to think I could do better,' she confessed. 'I have had to come to terms with the fact that I can't do everything perfectly. I set guidelines now for what I can do and accept help.'

Diana Green was motivated by a desire to prove herself. 'I had a nervous breakdown as a teenager and dropped out of university in the third year. Then I joined the civil service as a trainee and resigned after six years.' That's when she returned to university to do a PhD. 'I had a wobble, but I got over it and needed to prove to my family that I could do it.'

Heather MacDonald 'The feeling that success meant 100 per cent and not 99 per cent, the gold medal not the silver and being first in the work "race" every time. I eventually recognised the competitive perfectionist in me and that recognition helps, but I haven't overcome it and still set myself impossibly high standards.'

So your business career is up and running. You've tackled sexism. You've learned a bit about boardroom good practice and a lot about boardroom behaviour. You've done a personal stocktake to find out which aspects of your character need strengthening, and worked on overcoming weaknesses. Barriers come in all shapes and sizes and there have been plenty in your path, but you've brought them crashing down in your own inimitable style. Looks like you are set for success. Well, the bad news is we've barely started. You are still at the beginning of your journey into the business world. There's much more to discover from me and the businesswomen who have contributed to this book so, read on . . .

CHAPTER 2

Keeping the Hatchets from Your Head

We women talk too much, but even then we don't tell half what we know.
Nancy Astor, politician

Hold on to your hat so you don't make your neighbour a thief.
Old Iranian saying provided by Pooya Ahmadi

How do you feel about your work being plagiarised?

I'm not precious about ideas. **Christine Booth**

I have taken it as an indirect compliment when it has happened but I also remind people about the facts, in a nice way. **Sandra Brown**

Why do colleagues steal ideas from others and present them as their own? Now, I've got no statistics to back this up but I feel strongly women are ripped off more often than men. By and large women are more giving and willing to compromise. They also tend to be more compassionate and empathetic than male colleagues and so make ideal team players. These characteristics, coupled with a predisposition to share the glory and shoulder the blame, can mean less scrupulous employees take advantage of women bosses. At worst, after being forced to forego the triumphs they rightly deserve, women bosses can be subjected to downright abuse.

This section will help women spot the tell-tale signs of such scenarios before the hatchet falls.

Credit Where Credit's Due

I have always made a special effort to ensure that recognition is given when it's due. However, you won't be surprised to learn that in the business world this is far from the norm. Indeed my experience has shown me that it is the exception rather than the rule. Over the years I have gone out of my way to praise and reward, particularly those people whose ideas are duly adopted and help the company to prosper. By and large I have taken the brunt of the blame where there may be any inkling at all that I am responsible.

I am not saying this to make me appear like some superhero. It's the professional way to operate. But that's been scant consolation when

I have sat at a board table to hear someone else presenting my ideas as their own. Likewise, there's small comfort in having been ultra professional while being made the scapegoat when plans I have not put in place have gone awry. Both type of events have left a poisonous taste in my mouth as I am left to either share the accolade or bear the wrath.

My experience says that plagiarism is largely a male activity. Of course my own personal statistics could be skewed, not least because most of the managers and directors I have encountered have been men, but I can't recall a female colleague either taking the bouquet from or throwing the bat at the wrong parties.

My first business had a wonderful strapline I had used from day one: Building Better Businesses. No clever marketing man had created this – it had been entirely a Jo Haigh invention and I had put it all over my brochures, letterheads and so forth. I worked closely with a local government-sponsored training organisation at the time and to my horror they developed a programme that didn't directly involve me and branded it – Building Better Businesses.

I've lost count of the times I have suggested a solution or method of working, which has then been presented as someone else's innovation. Only the other day I gave a colleague an idea about presenting a particular activity during a training event. Then, with me standing next to him, he told the delegates he had just had a great idea on how to run the next session. He couldn't look me in the eye; it was unbelievably shabby behaviour. However, some interviewees found women to be the villains in this arena.

Have you been the victim of plagiarism?

Rosemary Conley 'Someone impersonated me and a mail-order catalogue used my name to endorse their product without my accreditation.'

Tracy Viner 'I have worked with bullies and lots of plagiarisers, particularly women. For a while I overlooked it until I couldn't tolerate it any more so I started to by-pass that person on the basis that life is too short . . .'

Sarah Deaves 'I once worked for a woman who took credit for all my ideas over and over again. It was very frustrating and upsetting but I never let it show at work. I found ways to get round her, to show my own stuff to the people who mattered. And I vowed never to be like that with any of my staff.'

Deborah Adshead 'It is mostly female bosses who have done this, often in a subtle way. I felt it petty to point out what had occurred – I'm a non-confrontational person – so I let it go. Now I have learned to keep back the best of my ideas to present personally.'

Anon One anonymous contributor holds that plagiarism happens a lot, and the higher up the corporate ladder you climb, the more prevalent it becomes. It's an issue spanning both sexes, although for different reasons. 'Women tend to be jealous,' says Gail Carter, owner of Business Support Services, 'and men chauvinistic.'

Dianne Sharp 'Once, when I was in a finance role, I spoke to the operations director about my ideas, he then presented them as his own at the next board meeting. I let him get on with it, waiting until he tripped himself up, and I learned a valuable lesson about who to trust.'

Alexis Cleveland At the heart of the Cabinet Office, Alexis works in a highly charged political atmosphere where intellectual theft is far from remarkable. She has witnessed other people professing her ideas, then floundering as they are unable to carry the project through. She pursues a softly-softly approach: 'If I can I will throw in a line to indicate that it was my idea in the first place and add value to it. But I try not to make enemies as I progress.'

Naturally there are advantages to taking credit where it is not honestly due. The plagiariser will eventually achieve the rewards attached to a successful idea – and these aren't just necessarily financial. Of course disadvantages also exist when taking credit where it's not honestly due, your own personal sense of guilt not being the least of them, along with shame and the hurt you cause to the real advocate. Don't forget that you may be found out, and that is unlikely to be career enhancing. Just as likely is the fact that if you do take credit for an idea that isn't truly yours, you may be asked to implement it and not only is it highly possible you won't have the skills, but you may find it very difficult to get the support you need.

However, while policy theft may not make the perpetrator Mr Popular with you, that is not their aim. I have dealt with some severely delusional people who genuinely believe the initial idea was theirs and would be affronted if you were to challenge this assumption.

If your ideas are being stolen from under your nose then office politics can escalate. Fiona Cruickshank admits she doesn't have a sensitive nature: 'I always feel flattered but irritated beyond belief when people steal ideas. I don't get mad, I get even.' Helen Merfield, CEO of Health and Case Management Limited, sees plagiarism as a challenge: 'When my ideas have been taken I have come up with something better and more innovative. I wouldn't tolerate being put down and would react with a witty one-liner.'

PLAGIARISM SURVIVAL GUIDE

If you encounter such behaviour in the early days of your career being carried out by someone in a senior position it's a very difficult call. I would recommend to you the following:

- Don't just let it pass!

- Be cautious about dealing with this head-on in front of others, particularly because it could be humiliating to the senior player.

- Using your best non-threatening manner, tackle the perpetrator on a one-to-one basis.

- State what you think happened.

- Provide justification for your stance.

- Ask for the rationale for their statement.

- Get agreement for an appropriate restatement of the 'true' position.

In my experience most men are very proud and you need to negotiate this tricky territory with care. If you are the junior player it will be very important in 99 per cent of cases for the man not to lose face. But don't let it pass! If it has happened once and you didn't deal with the issue, it will happen again. A similarly strong stance is needed if you are served up on a plate as the agitator/protagonist, though clearly if this were a very serious matter with potential disciplinary or worse consequences you may want to document your position. Such confrontations are usually best avoided, but if you have to go there, go there.

Confrontation

Any similar situation with peers and subordinates should be dealt with in the same manner if you want to minimise confrontation. A formula of reprimanding in private and praising in public has always stood me in good stead. Tempting as it may be to go for the jugular, losing your rag is rarely an attractive or career-enhancing trait. It's forgivable only in exceptional circumstances.

If such activity continues, you could try a subtle approach directly in public, perhaps something like this: 'That's such a great idea, when I mentioned it to X last week, we agreed it would be difficult to find a better alternative.' You may even continue, 'In fact, when I first thought of it I believed we had hit on a perfect solution.' If neither of these strategies achieve the desired result and you feel strongly enough about it, make sure influential players are made aware of just whose ideas are being adopted. The office grapevine can be effective, but operate in this minefield with care.

While bearing in mind all of the above, I'm grateful to other women survivors for suggesting a different approach.

**Heather MacDonald, principal and chief executive
of Wakefield College**

I take it as a compliment if my ideas are plagiarised by others. As I work in a large public-sector organisation with a shared mission and corporate goals, achieving the latter is the key to our success.

There are, as Angela Hughes, commercial director of JVL Products Limited, points out, bigger things in life than scoring brownie points. And Dr Jane Guise, CEO of the Royal Bath & West of England Society, has recognised that there is no room for pride when it comes to company success. Fay Sharpe, director and shareholder of Zibrant, is rarely denied the merit that's due to her. 'I'm strong enough to stand by my beliefs in everything I do so I will always speak up.' By the same token she also offers praise where it's due. 'Don't take credit for other people's great ideas. Let them showcase their talent – it builds trust and respect in your team.'

Sometimes problems come from a surprising source. Jayne Doherty, MD of Joyce Estate Agents, recalls how her father, a silent partner in her estate agency business, took credit for her successes. 'I got used to it, but it was annoying at times. It's a guy thing. I pat myself on the back as no one else does it.'

Compromise

Achieving a compromise is not the same as backing down or giving in, yet many men in senior positions view any movement on their original stance as a sign of weakness. When you have a management team or board where the male/female numbers are unevenly spread in favour of men, my experience is that women will do one of two things: stand their corner or offer a compromise for the sake of a swift solution. The latter tactic often accelerates the process (assuming the compromise is accepted, of course). Sometimes it's just not appropriate but appears the only realistic action.

So should women continue to compromise and keep offering the olive branch when our male colleagues are less inclined to do the same? Each case will have its own peculiarities and justification for moving towards the centre position so judgement will inevitably be on a situation by situation basis.

Once again I advise against indulging in the mother of all hissy fits because it always seems to be you who has to back down. Instead, try some of the following tactics.

Remain Silent

One of the best negotiating tactics I have found is to remain silent after you have made your case. This can be very powerful and ushers in a situation where the other side has to keep talking to justify their position. I have found opponents often talk themselves into a corner. But for many women, including me, the silent part is very difficult.

On average a woman speaks approximately three times more words a day than a man and, if you are like me at all, you are sometimes rushing ahead so quickly that you are refuting something before hearing the whole scenario.

Listen

Recently I learned a fabulous technique called 'active listening'.

Get a colleague to describe something to you for about five minutes. Then try paraphrasing back to them the real essence of what they said. If you do this exercise properly you will notice a couple of things: in order to stay focused you have to stay quiet; you want to hear what they are *actually* saying, not what you think they *may* say. Knowing you will have to paraphrase means you concentrate on the true content rather than just picking up the gist – often entirely different matters.

Once you get into the swing of doing this you will not only gain hugely improved listening skills but by understanding what is being said and repeating it back you show a much greater insight into the issue in question. Using this technique you will also be much more effective in gaining compromise. Being the peacemaker is not a weak role. Someone competent in this area can gain respect and prevent inertia, but don't expect these skills to come naturally, without any effort.

Little Wins

A final tactic I have found useful is to make sure that 'little wins' are acknowledged as you go through the process. For instance, in a pay negotiation you may say, 'OK, I accept that to give the award in March is premature but can we agree July is a reasonable target?' You may have to try various methods to get a desired result. Remember the mantra: if you do what you've always done, you get what you've always got!

When Pooya Ahmadi, CEO of the Business Channel, was struggling to make her business a success, she asked friends and trusted advisors for help. She is an example to us all – when she has felt the cool breeze from a hatchet falling perilously close to her head she listened, learned and moved on.

So, when your ideas are stolen, although it feels akin to treachery, use the plan outlined above to regain a foothold on firm ground. It is not the time to throw the teddies out of the pram, no matter how tempting an option that may seem. Stay cool, learn from mistakes made and do everything possible to ensure the same outrage doesn't happen again.

CHAPTER 3

Work/Life Balance: Fact or Fiction?

My second favourite household chore is ironing. My first one being hitting my head on the top bunk bed until I faint.
Erma Bombeck, comedian

I'm not going to vacuum till Sears makes one you can ride on.
Roseanne Barr, actor

I am woman! I am invincible! I am pooped!
Anon

What's your best advice to achieve a work/life balance?

I go home early if I get stressed, and bump people from my diary. I work fast and set deadlines for jobs. **Christine Booth**

Prioritise well, decide what you want and go for it. It's easy to get burnt out if you don't. **Jayne Doherty**

Make time for the kids. If you need to work at home, do it after they have gone to bed. **Barbara Harvey**

I compartmentalise my time. I have odd pangs of guilt, but I accept that I'm not perfect. **Deirdre Bounds**

Don't be possessive about your children. **Alison Boxall**

Be meticulously organised. **Anon**

Plan a social life so that work does not take over. **Fiona Vanstone**

Appreciate the first three years will be very difficult. Learn how to switch off. **Deborah Adshead**

We all like to think we're superhuman but if you don't get rid of the guilt and ask for help with the household chores, you'll soon burn out. **Anon**

I learned early on that long hours don't necessarily achieve all you want. I start early and always leave on time. **Helen Merfield**

Think about how you would advise someone you cared about. Focus on what really matters. **Jeanette Sargent**

Take no work home at the weekends. **Alexis Cleveland**

Don't be a slave to routine. **Dr Jane Guise**

Learn how to relax. **Nicole Paradise**

Most women have a caring gene that is more visible than in the male of the species. It applies to those who are married with children and to singletons. Of course there are millions of kind and generous men but, by and large, women are the homemakers and carers. Inevitably this can create conflict with a business workload. Most women multi-task as second nature; an art that still eludes most men. There's a phrase that springs to mind: 'If you want something done, ask a busy woman.' For, no matter how much she accrues on her 'to do' list, her routine goals are usually accomplished.

This section of the book provides coping techniques and tips supported by anecdotes from the contributors.

Caring, Sharing, Homemaking

Nobody objects to a woman being a good writer or sculptor or geneticist if at the same time she manages to be a good wife, a good mother, good-looking, good-tempered, well-dressed, well-groomed, and unaggressive.
Marya Mannes, author

Over the years I have tried very hard to separate my home life from my work life with varying degrees of success. After all, do we work to live or live to work? For the most part (there have been some exceptions), I have been very fortunate. I have had jobs I've thoroughly enjoyed and most mornings I have arrived at work looking forward to the day. In fact, sad as it sounds, after my two-week annual holiday I am generally itching to get back to the office. However, my home and my family are considerably more important than my work. Although I have made huge compromises in attempting to attain my career goals I always put family first. Fortunately, I don't have to make a choice between them, although sometimes women are made to feel they do.

Many professional women aim to have it all: a beautiful home and an immaculate garden; to host wonderful parties; attend school plays and parents' evenings; to be well dressed and groomed; to be an attentive wife and mother; to bake buns and help with homework. I've run myself into the ground trying to tick all those boxes, while attempting to remain the same alluring woman my husband married. Oh, and delivering on time on all job requirements from sourcing new clients to getting the best deal in town.

Of course this is an impossible task for any one person. This is the job of at least four or five people including a gardener, PA, house-keeper and nanny.

Many women multi-task at this level, but even the best of jugglers will occasionally drop a ball, or the high-wire artist will miss a step and fall (hopefully) into the safety net. Where no safety net exists – that's usually a financial safety net provided by a legacy or a partner – the outcome can often be a nervous or physical breakdown.

Every working mother will understand the all-encompassing guilt we suffer all the time. When we are at work we miss our child's nativity play. When we are at the play we miss the critical client meeting. And when your child is sick, what do you do then?

Of course it's not just offspring who cause these insufferable dilemmas, it could just as easily be siblings or parents. And it's not that my husbands (both of them) haven't cared about our children or family, or even our home, it's just that men seem better able to compartmentalise their lives so none of the above becomes a major issue.

One possible advantage the male species seems to have over the female is that they are able to do just one thing at a time. Consequently, they give that one thing 100 per cent of their attention and have a tendency to be extraordinarily thorough. It gives them a competitive edge.

How many women reading this will spend their lunch hour shopping for supper, picking up the dry cleaning and booking the holiday while pondering problems in the office? I have a pad and pen by my bed to jot down the 1001 things I think of in those twilight hours between sleep and that brain-numbing alarm at 6 a.m. We have all put on our lipstick (and the rest) at the traffic lights when running late after a mammoth effort to find the hockey stick/football/books lost by James or Jemima before breakfast. Reluctant though I am to speak for the whole of womankind, I think I can generalise a bit about working women. Like me, you have undoubtedly left numerous events and meetings prematurely to deal with some domestic crisis. (I once took a telephone call during a business conference from my daughter, telling me the bathroom was on fire and that she was putting it out. Although she told me not to worry, I still did!) Like me, you have been racked with guilt on numerous occasions. Yet the difficult decision to depart in order to counter a crisis on the home front has probably been greeted with varying responses from smirking or seething to downright abuse from those colleagues left behind. Like me, you may have turned down dream job opportunities in the knowledge that the travel or responsibility would be so onerous as to prevent you comfortably coping with your domestic duties.

The question is, would a man consider this before making a decision to up sticks and settle halfway across the country or even across the globe? Possibly. But they would rate problems on the home front lower down the list than women. My brother-in-law went to work in Hong Kong on a six-month secondment when his children were still at school. Five years later he was still there! Of course he couldn't have done that if my step-sister hadn't stayed at home in the UK to look after the family. Would a woman do as he did? I think it less likely.

So far, much reference has been made to looking after children, but all these points are just as applicable to ageing relations or even close friends.

If your very nature dictates an inclination towards the caring, sharing and homemaking then, frankly, it's fairly pointless to fly in the face of DNA.

Certainly, my own experiences have been tame compared with those of Julie Kenny, whose husband left when their children were eight, five and three.

CASE STUDY

Julie Kenny CBE, MD and founder shareholder of Pyronix Limited

'It took six years for the divorce to sort out all the financial matters. Unfortunately it wasn't amicable. We had a few days in court,' concedes Julie. She and her husband had started their business together, years before, selling everything including their home to do so. Until the birth of the children she worked as a secretary during the day and on the business until the early hours of the morning. Following the divorce she was alone with a business to run and three young children to care for. 'It was difficult not having anyone with whom to share the good and bad times. I was travelling a lot so I employed a daytime and night-time nanny. Even if I had employed a live-in, that person would still have needed time off.'

Ten years later she continues the long-held habit of making dates with the children once a month. 'They have a very special day each month with me, when they get to choose what we do. This is some personal time for them, giving us the opportunity to make a connection. When they were younger I also worked at home at night rather than the office so I was at close at hand.'

Recently she has been awarded a CBE for services to the voluntary sector, a practice she began to fill the gap after her husband left. 'Diverse perspectives from all the things I did have been a bonus. You can look at things a little more objectively. You have got to focus on what you want to achieve. You have got to believe that this is what you need to achieve. Surround yourself with good people. They help you get through it.'

With the hard-headed rationale and calculation of a business brain, she later decided to have her stomach stapled in order to lose weight, although before submitting to the operation she carried out extensive investigations.

I never had a problem with energy. I have always been able to work hard but now the exertion is easier. It is fantastic. It is nice not to be the fattest person in the room. And sometimes I was. I've been fat all my life. I do think there was an inherent prejudice against fatter children. Life was harder for them. Two generations later we are all slightly heavier so the issues have receded a bit.

I did a lot of research and went to talk to people who had it done. I watched the procedure on TV together with my children, who were involved in the decision making. One of the three wanted me to have a band rather than the more severe operation. But after the operation, this procedure was low maintenance so I chose it. It was painful but not unbearable.

In the end I looked at things from a business perspective. You need to weigh up risks and then make a decision and implement it. I might seem a little bit cold but that's how it was.

Afterwards she lost eight stones in eight months. Now, with a successful and fulfilling life behind her, she says: 'I'm the sum total of all my experiences. Life isn't a rehearsal. It is really about being focused and doing what you want to do.'

Nor has her progression through life come to a halt, despite her eventful existence to date. She always has either an educational or personal development book at her bedside. 'There isn't one book that copes with everything that comes your way in life. A lot of it is common sense. But we all carry on learning and the books are a kind of validation.'

The Enlightened Workplace

The family-friendly laws that have come into force in recent years, including extended maternity leave and dependent care leave, along with the right to flexible working, have meant that the more enlightened companies which have such advantageous working practices in place have set the benchmark for other employers to follow.

Some employers are golden examples of how the workplace should be. Google, with its 16,000 employees worldwide, is a much-vaunted illustration. On its website it gives a list of the top ten reasons to work for the company. In at number three is 'appreciation is the best motivation'. The workplace is 'fun and inspiring' with an on-site doctor and dentist, massage and yoga, professional development opportunities, child-care provision and delicious free food.

The philosophy that work and play are not mutually exclusive comes in at number four. At number five is 'We love our employees and we want them to know it' followed by 'Innovation is our bloodline' at number six.

With children welcome at the office, free bicycles and no one wearing a suit, it sounds like something out of la-la land. Yet the company is for real. Google CEO Eric Schmidt elaborates on the people-first policy on their website at www.google.com/intl/en/jobs:

> The goal is to strip away everything that gets in our employees way. We provide a standard package of fringe benefits, but on top of that are first-class dining facilities, gyms, laundry rooms, massage rooms, haircuts, carwashes, dry cleaning, commuting buses – just about anything a hardworking employee engineer might want. Let's face it: programmers want to program, they don't want to do their laundry. So we make it easy for them to do both.

And let's not forget that some 1,000 employees have made fortunes of $5 million plus thanks to stock options once offered as perks. Masseuse Bonnie Brown, Google's forty-first employee when she joined the start-up company in 1999, had no head for technology or flair with software. She was hired as a part-timer to improve the working conditions of the small band of people who breathed life into Google at the beginning of the internet revolution. Now she has made a fortune following the stock-market float of 2004 after which she converted most of her options into bundles of cash. The few she held on to continued to climb in value until shares hit an all-time record high that was 900 per cent above their debut price. If only modern-day fairy stories like this one happened more often.

Nonetheless, Wall Street-generated fortunes aside, imagine how much easier it would be to rocket up the ranks in a firm like this. Obviously, the benefits apply equally to men and women, but it is on mothers or carers they have the greatest impact. They have entirely defied the doubters who claimed the laws weighted towards the family make women less attractive to employers.

So what do the most far-sighted companies offer to female employees these days? To begin, what about paying for childcare facilities during out-of-area conferences, or offering time off to those undergoing fertility treatment? And there's more. Sue Day is a corporate finance manager at KPMG during working hours, but devotes her free time to women's rugby. Thanks to the generous time-off package she negotiated in 2007 she was able to captain England to a grand slam in the Six Nations tournament. In an interview for *The Times* on 3 October 2007, she said, 'It's easy for a big firm to make the right noises on flexible working but that has to be backed up by managers at a local level.'

And let's face it, there's an untold number of men just waiting for women to do battle on flexible working. That's because they also want to go to sports day or attend parents' evenings too, but struggle to vocalise that wish. When the war is won they'll reap the benefits and will be delighted to do so.

The most enlightened human resources departments will tell you that family-friendly policies result in a paring down of the absences people take illicitly to fulfil family obligations to a bare minimum.

But this coterie of companies that both embrace national and international law and have gone still further for the sake of their employees are not in the majority. I know many of you will have encountered a very different work ethos to that which prevails at Google in which lateness in leaving the office is valued more highly than genuine achievements scored between nine and five.

Legislation

The law which enshrines the rights of women workers is one thing but reality is an entirely different matter. When you are desperate to climb further up the corporate ladder, the actual process of taking up these legal rights is a difficult issue.

Frankly, even when you are at the top of your ladder, you still have an unenviable maintenance job to stay there, and it might still be a tall order to take advantage of these beneficial rights. Resorting to law grabs the headlines, but may not be the easiest way forward, either emotionally or career-wise.

One forty-year-old woman, who does not wish to be named, sued the bank she worked for in 2004. She says that despite the veneer of equal opportunities:

In many ways, things are worse now for women than they used to be. I remember when traders used to crawl under our desks to see if we were wearing stockings, but that was easy to deal with. The sexism has now gone underground and while several of the big banks look like they're making concerted efforts to recruit more women, in my experience, they're still not following through. It just makes it easier for them to fight cases when they can say: 'Look at our diversity training, we've ticked the box.' Any kind of work to redress inequality of any type should be applauded, but it needs to have teeth.

She settled out of court, but has not worked since her case. 'I genuinely think I would find it easier to tell someone I'm HIV positive than to tell them I have sued for sexual discrimination, the stigma is so strong,' she says. 'There's only one thing worse than suing a bank and that's winning,' says employment lawyer Gillian Howard. The vast majority of those women who win their cases never work in the City again; they become professional pariahs, losing large potential earnings. On the other hand, if they lose, the huge legal costs are life-changing.

Linda Davies has written about life at the top in *The Sunday Times*, and in an article on 4 September 1993 said:

Many of my female colleagues have since dropped out [of jobs in the City] voluntarily, while others have been forced out by recession, which has savaged men and women alike. But men find it easier to fire women than other men. They labour under the misapprehension that behind every City woman is an even richer man who will take care of her, whereas the men have no such safety net, being providers themselves.

Another reason for the disappearance from the City of many women is that they have collided with the glass ceiling. But I suspect that changed ambition, just as much as thwarted ambition, is behind their leaving. Money and status are worth little when you have to battle so hard to win them and barely have the time or the energy to enjoy them.

When the dependants are children there's a tunnel with light at the end of it. With only one teenager still at home (at one time or another I have had four or five if you count my husband!), I have more flexibility now than I ever had. I can stay out later, if I want to, although more often than not my daughter is out later than me, either working or partying. I can stay away overnight, or even nights, knowing she can look after herself, unmade beds, unwashed clothes and a filthy home notwithstanding. And I don't seem to have as many school activities to attend or to collect from. Of course it does help that she can now drive. (Then again, more anxiety and expense.)

Buying Help

With success comes the ability to 'buy' help. I am very fortunate as I have my own 'wife' in the form of a full-time housekeeper. This was an extravagance that at one time I couldn't really afford, but for the sake of my own sanity and that of other members of my family, we decided to make sacrifices elsewhere. When my children were little I had a live-in nanny, a great luxury. In the early days, after I had paid her, it was hardly worth working given the amount of money I could then call my own. But if someone was there for the children I had greater flexibility at work and significantly less anxiety about dealing with late meetings or childhood illnesses.

Today I have a wonderful team just a telephone call away that books my holidays, mows my lawns, does my food shopping and cleans my house. Yes, I am lucky I can afford such comforts. This is the way I choose to spend my income, as it affords me the chance to pursue the activities I love to do rather than those I have to do. But it certainly hasn't always been like that. For years I spent Saturday morning shopping, Sunday morning cleaning and ironing and Sunday afternoon fitting in all the other chores that had been left undone.

Coaching

One way of achieving a healthy work/life balance is through a coach. Not a sports coach, thankfully, but someone who peers into your daily life and suggests new approaches to achieve a more enjoyable existence. Sometimes it's just a case of tweaking existing habits, but the differences can be quantifiable and quick to achieve.

Mother of three Julia Hobsbawm ran a media analysis and networking business as well as holding down a demanding domestic routine. In 2007 she told *The Times*: 'I was buckling under the pressure and the guilt. I was too stressed, too preoccupied and too hyped up to cope with the demands of small children.' As a result, she used to hang back at the office after a twelve-hour day rather than embrace the minutiae of family life. Then she consulted a coach and, in common with many other CEOs and high-fliers, discovered a new route less bumpy than the original.

I have 25 per cent less guilt and 25 per cent more productivity. In the office I am making strategic decisions that are bolder and making them quicker. And when I walk through the door at the end of the day I know how to put work to one side. I don't want to make out I have completely cracked it, but I no longer feel that my life is out of control.

The coaching industry is booming in America where a survey by the Chartered Institute of Personnel and Development found that 63 per cent of its members have a coach. Remember, this is not therapy. Coaches steer clear of the emotional baggage and concentrate only on the nuts and bolts of the hamster wheel. It's not cheap but it might be worth it.

Techniques and Tips for Coping

No woman is required to build the world by destroying herself.
Rabbi Sofer

Not everyone can afford such comforts or they may choose to spend their hard-earned income in other ways, finding different coping strategies. By and large we do cope, with varying degrees of success. I admit that this ongoing guilt trip and the sheer exhaustion of trying to be all things to all people has driven me on too many occasions to the wine bottle at the end of the day. Sometimes I have even sought prescription medicine to relax. Neither has proven to be a long-term solution. However, if you've been there too, rest assured you are in the majority, not the minority.

If you feel it's a sin to ask for help, be it practical or medical, take it from someone who has been stumbling around in the fog of daily life that it really isn't. The help I have received when I've been at breaking point has undoubtedly saved me from shattering into little pieces. I'm going to look at coping techniques and tips. The use of these depends entirely on individual circumstance, your own preferences and, to an extent, financial circumstances.

Delegate

I accepted long, long ago I am a control freak and that's not going to change. This particular personality trait makes it very difficult for me to abdicate responsibility for virtually anything, but I have learned to delegate in a fashion, which helps me enormously. Very simply, I will delegate tasks, but I keep a running list (yes, an actual written list) of everything I have asked someone to do, be it my husband, my PA, my housekeeper or a colleague. Sad, very sad, I know, but it works for me so don't knock it! This has allowed me to solicit help in my own controlled manner. Where funds allow, I buy help, be it from gardeners, nannies, housekeepers or personal assistants.

The internet has provided working women with much greater flexibility. The discovery of online shopping has changed many women's lives, although I have had some interesting experiences when one satsuma arrived instead of the bag I thought I had ordered and the 144 tins of dog food that came instead of the fourteen I was expecting! My miniature Yorkshire terrier was as bemused as the delivery man, who asked if I ran kennels.

Lists

I am a great list maker even to the extent of writing things down just to cross them off. It fills me with a sense of satisfaction, albeit brief. Not just shopping lists, though clearly these are essential, but all sorts of lists and plans. My husband bought me a beautiful little notebook embossed with the words 'Dreams and Thoughts' and my initials. I keep it in my handbag and have divided it into my own particular categories. I have a running shopping list and a 'to do' list, and also a longer-term wish list.

With four children, I keep a list whenever they mention anything they would like, so when it comes to birthdays I can get them something they really want instead of wondering what to buy. I have a list pinned on my noticeboard of all the people I buy birthday presents for and, in the last few years, I have been out in the January sales to buy all or most of their presents and cards. Please don't vomit when I tell you that I have immediately wrapped and labelled them, ready to give out on the due date. This has saved me running around at the last minute, and buying in the sales has meant I have been able to be more generous than otherwise. I buy Christmas presents and label them throughout the year for the same reasons.

My holidays have always kept me sane and not only do I put them in my diary twelve months in advance but I book them as far in advance as funds allow.

I realise these methods of management will not suit everyone, but they work for me and that's what's important. I'm simply not a last-minute sort of girl. If you are, then good for you but, in order to multi-task at optimum levels, I have to forward plan.

I was delighted to discover that Rosemary Conley, the diet guru, and I were sounding the same drum beat for working women. Here's her tip for achieving a work/life balance:

Determine your goals and write them down: short, medium and long term, including business and personal ones.

I was trained as a secretary and knew how to run an office, and then I became a Tupperware lady. Both these jobs taught me that I had two strengths: how to be good presenter and how to be good on the phone. I am a born organiser. Women tend to try and do too much as well as looking after the family. Take advice and read books and learn from others who have succeeded. When I worked for a multinational company, which I did for more than four years, it was all about the bottom line, whereas we want people to be satisfied first and foremost, and provide a good service. I work with my husband now and love running our business.

Support at Home

Support on the domestic front has a significant impact on job satisfaction for many women. 'I have a great, supportive husband who gave up his career for me,' explains Natalie Douglas. 'I try to get a work/life balance, but during the week work comes first. Weekends, however, are sacrosanct. My tip is to compartmentalise your weekend time.'

If you are married or have a partner you should of course be able to rely on them. It sounds like Rosemary has got that one cracked. But on a practical basis I have found this to be pretty much a non-starter. You may, of course, be more fortunate than me and, if so, make the most of it! But if your partner or husband is similar to mine, well, I have found clear, unambiguous instruction rather than polite requests achieves the best results.

You may even recruit help from among those dependants who are causing you the problem in the first place. As children we all had our jobs on a Saturday whether it was cleaning the bathroom or hoovering. Frankly, I would be satisfied if my children kept the floor of their rooms free of sweet papers and laundry. For my children, bribery works. I'm sure you will find your own methods.

Acceptance

If you are very driven there is little point me telling you that it's not possible to do everything really well. You won't believe me and, who knows, perhaps you are right. I have always struggled with wanting to be the best and finding myself falling short. With some nightmare times behind me, I advise you just do the best you can and keep sane by whatever means works for you.

Perween Warsi, founder and chief executive of S & A Foods

The single hardest thing to achieve in business is to strike a balance between work and family life. It's something I have had to work at along the way. I am lucky to have an incredibly supportive husband and family, who are as passionate about the business as I am.

In the early days my two sons were still young. When I was setting up the business the hours were very demanding and I had to split myself between being at home for my sons and my husband and giving my business the best chance. This meant me working very long hours, both at the factory and at home. Some days I worked an eighteen- or twenty-hour day, making sure everything was done.

I think determination is the key. I was determined that my family wouldn't suffer but I was also determined to kick-start my business in the best way possible. In the end my family were the key to the success of my business and my business the key to the success of my family. But it takes sheer hard work and determination to do both.

One woman, a mother of four, told me how her family commitments are viewed as a negative at the corporation she works for. However, if a man announces his intention to attend the school sports day or play he is applauded for his modern outlook. The struggle to balance work and home life is felt among most women executives.

How do you achieve a good work/life balance?

Sarah Deaves has recognised there is no perfect solution to the work/life balance. Still, she believes that doesn't mean you can't enjoy both. It's a question of working out an arrangement with which you are comfortable. 'Recognise that each time a new phase in the home life occurs, like starting school, you face new challenges. Don't lose sight of the fact that these are primarily great fun and bring you joy. The balancing act never ends but there is always a way through.'

Rolline Frewen believes that keeping your promises at home and at work means never having to feel guilty about going to the office. 'Ensure the agreed times and days spent at home (or work) are kept to. Both office and family can organise their lives around you and everyone knows when and where you are for them. At the end of it all the husband and children will respect you for working.'

Anita Brough 'I had my children young and have always involved them. We eat as a family whenever we can. I am realistic about what is possible and what isn't. I got my kids to help in the house from the start.'

Pinky Lilani 'Work will always be there in different ways. However, your children will grow up and leave – and that period of your life can never come back.'

Kitchen Table Tycoons

For some women, the arrival of children is a spur to greatness at work. In the recent past the emotional roller-coaster of childbearing proved to be a dark time for some women in business, Sonita Alleyne, CEO of Somethin' Else, among them. 'I had a tough time when I came back [to work] through lack of empathy, particularly through the transition between home and work. I felt I was in a battlefield, I felt isolated.' Too many women felt it was a straight choice between baby and business. But now the lines are increasingly blurred, as my research has discovered.

Many women who have already succeeded in business before giving up work to become mothers are dissatisfied. Finding it impossible to let their sound business brains idle, they start home-based companies that fit better with their family-orientated lifestyles. Kitchen table tycoons have set up businesses with annual sales of nearly £4.5 billion, according to the London School of Economics.

A famous example is Friends Reunited, the website dreamed up by Julie Pankhurst in 1999 when she was expecting her first child. She was wondering what her old school friends were doing, whether they had families and where they lived. With help from her husband, Steve, she embarked on the innovative dot.com idea at their home in Barnet, north London. The business was recently sold for £175 million.

Nearly three-quarters of women who started a business after they gave birth did so when their child was less than two years old. These mumtrepreneurs often start baby-related businesses like importing baby goods but also include stay at home sectors like marketing, accounting and web design.

Hannah Evans, founder of Piccalilly

I had decided to set up Piccalilly about one month after the birth of my second daughter, Cicely. I was on maternity leave and I had just found out that I was probably going to be made redundant. My main hurdle was finding time to work while having a baby. At this stage I had no childcare and no means to pay for childcare. However, I had a huge amount of work to get things set up. The new business venture absorbed about ten months of development time, including trips to India to source wholesale suppliers.

I overcame the problems by working unconventional hours – evenings, very early mornings and weekends. Still to this day I occasionally work these patterns as they fit well with my overseas suppliers and also my customer base – who are predominantly women with children working from home.

How did you cope when you had a young child?

We're all proud of our offspring, but for years working women have been forced to bury those natural feelings for the sake of success at work. Now times are changing. It's no longer presumed that loving mums will be workplace disasters. Indeed, common sense says that a woman who can organise a briefcase and a baby is a sure-fired asset. While leaving spit-up on a suit is going a step too far, there's no reason to camouflage your family in these far more enlightened times.

Gail Carter Young mum and sole trader Gail Carter refused to let motherhood get in the way of her new business. She was establishing herself by becoming a familiar face at relevant business events, honing her public-relations skills and building contacts. 'When I had a small baby I arranged meetings around feed times and took my baby everywhere!'

Fay Sharpe 'Don't be afraid to lay down guidelines of when you can work. A good boss will respect that – there is no shame in having a life. However, when you are at work put your all into being focused. Don't waste time, plan your week and that way you'll feel OK about leaving on time.'

Fiona Sheridan Following the birth of a daughter, Fiona Sheridan reduced her working week to four days. After trying to cloak the fact for a while she is now certain the best approach is to be direct and honest. 'Set clear protocols on how you want to be, be open about it and tell everyone. I made a mistake by not telling people I was working four days a week. Start the way you mean to go on.'

Time Management

Any businesswoman, with or without children, knows the value of time management. Fortunately, it's a message that's getting through to everyone in the commercial world at the moment. Those macho habits of arriving first in the office and remaining there until the wee small hours are, I hope, largely behind us. After all it's quality of work achieved in the office that counts. And none of us are automatons. We all work better, faster and more creatively after a spot of well-deserved rest and recuperation.

Burning the midnight oil in the office is not always productive. Helen Merfield puts a successful life/work balance down to two assets: a great PA and an understanding husband. When she plans days off so her family can be together she earmarks them as sacred.

Another contributor felt that time can be squandered in the office. 'Don't work all the time. No one will notice or thank you for it and your best, most creative and big-picture ideas are likely to come while you are not working.' Alison Kennedy, programme manager and trainer at Salford University and 4C Change Limited, thinks you should 'Decide the latest time you will leave the office each day and stick to it. Two hours before the agreed time, if it is a really busy day, reschedule or reprioritise tasks so that it can happen. I haven't always followed my own advice but I've tried!' Another interviewee, Nicola Kay of Camden Electronics Limited, is frank about her failure to follow her own heartfelt advice: 'Restrict yourself to a nine-to-five day and be determined to stick to it. I wish I could! When I did this I know I worked better, felt happier and had a better social life.' According to Anne Lockwood, MD of First Choice Select Limited, the length of the working day is in your own hands:

I believe that if you constantly work overtime or long hours you are either overworked – which you can do something about – or inefficient. Therefore my one tip would be to achieve total efficiency and get off home. After all, everyone should have something to look forward to in their private lives, be it a night in with a glass of wine and a good book, a weekend away, time with friends or family. Plan it and do it.

For Angela Hughes, commercial director of JVL Products Limited, home is a refuge and it is important to spend time there, recuperating from her efforts at work. She also admits to being a meticulous planner, making dates as far into the future as is feasible. Time management, she insists, is essential.

Know Your Limits

You can't be all things to all people, so don't even try. It's in a woman's nature to tick as many boxes as she can find in a broad array of activities. Well, down that road lies a nervous breakdown. Recognise your limitations and stay within them. There are no rules here so don't be concerned about breaking any. There's no one waiting with a gold medal at the finishing line – although sometimes it feels like there should be. And what works for other women may not work for you.

Sue Catling, a previous parliamentary candidate for the Conservative Party, admits the work/life balance is a race that can't be won. 'Recognise that it is impossible to be a perfect partner, lover, mum, businesswoman, daughter, friend and so forth all by yourself and all at the same time, no matter how much stamina, talent and drive you possess. So don't try to be all these things. You'll exhaust yourself and underperform at everything. Delegate what you reasonably can at work and buy yourself as much help as you can possibly afford at home.'

Tracy Viner, owner and MD of her own company, finds it hard to compartmentalise. 'I find I am better if I don't separate my work persona from my home persona, as the whole is greater than two halves. I have fantastic friends who are very important to me as I am single, but I still have to give myself permission for time out.' Barbara Harvey, Assistant Dean at Sheffield Hallam University, also concedes the work/life balance is difficult. 'I have no time for myself because I strive all the time to be perfect. I have the "give us more work" ethic and am driven to succeed, to be as good as I can be. I do mix my work and home life. I think feedback helps you do a better job.'

Justine Dignam, of the Media Management Group, has unusual

advice: 'Learn to bake. I bake every weekend for my children who are at home during the week. I work 200 miles away from them, in London. There's no such thing as the perfect balance and the higher up you go doesn't mean it gets easier. I don't miss the momentous times but I know my salary is essential.' Another contributor advises: 'Don't try to be the best at everything. Just do your best. We all like to think we're superhuman but if you don't get rid of the guilt and ask for help with the household chores you'll soon burn out. That's no good for the business or the home.'

When Work Is a Priority

Sometimes work is at the top of the list of priorities. It just is. That may be because an order is being rushed through to meet a deadline or a presentation is being drawn up for a potential client. Whatever the reason, it's impossible to compartmentalise when it is occupying three-quarters of your brain space. It's at times like these you must be honest with yourself and your family. Earmark some time in the future to make you feel better about working around the clock now.

Christina Vaughan, CEO and Founder of Image Source Limited, puts career squarely at the top of her priorities. 'A lot of people talk about balance but all I understand is that if you have a dream of a vision and a desire to realise that then you must focus on the end game in order not to disappoint yourself.' She concedes that priorities change as time goes on. The arrival of children, for example, may make it necessary to seek more time off. But she thinks that for some women a career is a form of destiny that brings its own rewards: 'It is my belief that if we are doing what we are meant to do in life, if we always remain grounded with our roots deeply entrenched, everything will ultimately balance itself out. Finding one's vocation in life is a true privilege.'

Anon, joint owner of an IT solutions and support business

In life we make choices and we have to live with them. Choosing a career means making sacrifices in other areas of your life, just as choosing not to work would have a financial impact on the home life. Working full-time or – in the case of building a new business – full-time and a half, means that the home won't be as sparkling as it once was and someone else has to pick up the kids from school. But no one forces us to do this. That's the great thing about living in the UK. We can choose to stay home – or not.

So take ownership of the choice you make and don't feel guilty for not being able to do everything. Either way, something has got to give. Shop online to avoid the supermarkets and the malls. If you can, install a web-cam and have ten minutes chatting to the kids when they get home from school, from wherever you are in the world. Teach the rest of the family how to use the washer and dishwasher and get a cleaner, even if it's only once a month, to get your house back into tip-top shape.

One suggestion by Lesley Cowley, CEO of Nominet UK, has the whiff of controversy about it but nonetheless works for me: 'Interview for a supportive husband or partner with the same rigour that you would apply to a very senior appointment. Then ensure you listen when they tell you to stop.'

But if you think all of the above is too negative then revel in the words of Pooya Ahmadi who believes, quite simply, that you can have it all. Indeed, her positive mindset helps her move mountains. 'I strive to have it all every day although I don't always achieve it. But weekends are strictly no work and there's no evening work either. Nor do I expect it from employees. I lead by example.'

It's obvious that everyone is juggling furiously, whether they are mothers, wives or business executives. Sometimes I wonder if women are driving themselves into a lonely and senseless existence. Businesswoman Nicky Pattinson uses the caring and sharing nature of women as a powerful business tool. Remember, this was the woman who made a million out of a market stall. Why does she think people kept coming back? 'Every customer we served we gave them a chunk of us,' she explained. This might have been in the form of a conversation or a confidence, a brush of the wrist or a wink. 'It was validation, affirmation and affection,' she said. 'They were guests in our kitchen. Every single person got shown a little love that they probably weren't getting anywhere else in their lives.' Don't live life so fast and hard that the emotional and spiritual sides of your life are eroded. Create a little time and space just for you, as a reward for all of your hard work. Find the schedule that suits you and accept it might not mirror the one that your best buddy operates with astonishing success. Aim to satisfy each aspect of your life, for example, work, family, mind, fitness, self-maintenance and relaxation. Don't skimp on those subjects that come further down the list. As Diana Green of Sheffield Hallam University points out, life is not a rehearsal.

WORK/LIFE BALANCE SURVIVAL GUIDE

■ If you get the chance, choose your workplace carefully. Look for signs of enlightened management, happy faces and a centrally sited coffee machine. Should you encounter anyone crying in the toilets or spot people rocking backwards and forwards on their office chairs, go elsewhere.

■ Consider coaching to find a successful recipe for a work/life balance.

■ Buy in help. It's hard to be nanny, housekeeper, cook and chief executive all at the same time. Farm out some of the tasks to which you are less suited.

■ Make lists so that nothing slips under the daily radar.

■ Be proud of being a parent or a caring sibling or offspring. It's not something to be ashamed of.

■ Never miss your child's play, nativity or school event, you will never get a second chance.

■ Don't feel guilty if you eat the odd takeaway or use convenience food.

■ Just as you pledge time to the office, do the same to those at home. Keep your promises so you cannot be charged with preferring work to family.

■ Take holidays, even if it's time at home, and plan them in advance so you have something to look forward to.

■ Know your limits and don't exceed them. Being superwoman is old hat.

CHAPTER 4

Office Couture –
Make it Work for You

Inside me lives a skinny woman crying to get out.
But I can usually shut the bitch up with cookies.
Unknown

Remember, Ginger Rogers did everything Fred Astaire did,
but she did it backwards and in high heels.
Bob Thaves, cartoonist

How should you dress for work?

On business I usually wear Western dress. At home I sometimes wear more traditional Asian clothing. You have to be confident and comfortable in what you're wearing. **Perween Warsi**

Dress appropriately for what you do. **Joy Kingsley**

Dress to the expectation of your peers. **Justine Dignam**

Dress as you feel comfortable and in what's appropriate for the environment. **Deirdre Bounds**

Create your own personal style. I'm lucky to work in a creative environment. How I dress is an expression of myself. **Julia Moir**

I mix designer with high street, but ultimately people judge me on the way I present myself and I acknowledge that presentation is part of being a female entrepreneur. **Christina Vaughan**

Be memorable for style not fashion sense. **Lesley Cowley**

Don't expect staff to look smart if you are not. **Rolline Frewen**

Safer to play safe. **Yvonne Lumley**

I love the idea of breaking down stereotypes so dress accordingly. **Hannah Evans**

Be proud of yourself and stand out. **Barbara Scandrett**

Posture and body language or movement is important as is grooming and dressing in a stylish but sensual way. **Julia Gash**

Some women think it's a sin to look feminine after they reach a senior professional position. The message seems to be that, if we want to compete in a man's world, we must look like men. Well, it isn't a man's world and we don't have to be masculine to succeed. My own daughter, training as a lawyer in a large national firm, was given strict dress guidelines in what was and was not acceptable. This policy was poised to turn a beautiful twenty-two-year-old into a grey android. Of course, she could hardly flounce into a courtroom in frills or floppy hats, that's not what I am suggesting. There is a middle road regarding clothes and couture that beckons us all.

This chapter will not advocate revealing your décolletage (well, not all the time) but will consider what's acceptable, what's not and why, when and how to stand out.

Dress for Success

As a self-confessed shopaholic, I love – no, I absolutely adore – clothes, as well as jewellery, make-up, handbags . . . and, of course, shoes. I have a dream that one day shoe shops will be sited within the walls of all the major corporations. My husband has stopped asking me the inevitable question, 'Just how many handbags do you need?' The answer comes by way of another question. Just how many is too many!

But my love of shopping and clothes is one thing, dressing appropriately in business is entirely another. Coco Chanel said, 'Dress shabbily and they will notice the dress, dress impeccably and they will notice the woman.' How true is that? Come on, don't tell me you haven't made that comparison, if not in work then when you are socialising. After all, nobody wants their first impression to be their worst impression. But if impeccable dressing is a given, there's still room for creativity and imagination.

Heather MacDonald, principal and chief executive of Wakefield College, believes that dressing well helps you feel good about yourself. 'Being a chief executive does not have to equate to a pinstriped-suit image. Be confident about colour. The image you present has a subliminal effect on those you are trying to do business with or influence.'

What I have noticed, particularly in professional circles, is the tendency of many women to dress so soberly they could be going to a funeral. Now come on, we all love black, the most flattering and forgiving of colours, but appropriate trimming and accessories can change that drab, formal or androgynous look into something so much more stunning if you just take a few risks.

I hear the chorus of 'buts' already. Wearing a pretty floral dress and strappy sandals doesn't say professional and able – maybe it doesn't, but there is a compromise. I have always thought you should dress to please yourself. Wear what makes you happy and comfortable and above all what makes you confident. If confidence comes with an eighties power suit – go for it. If you feel better in a more dress-down ensemble then don't be afraid of choosing that particular outfit.

Lynda Hinxman, Assistant Dean at Sheffield Hallam University, stresses the importance of not looking like a man: 'I wear nice jewellery, long earrings and I like to be fairly glamorous – but not over the top,' she cautions. 'Look smart, be confident,' says Rosemary Conley. 'I have clothes that say I respect myself. Invest in a colour and style consultation to help prevent mistakes.'

Sue Catling, aspiring politician

While a place of business is rarely the location to experiment with high fashion, your dress and self-presentation should reflect the level or role you wish to achieve. In my case, it was being a member of parliament.

I always wore the basic 'uniform' for the occasion but added an individual twist. So when women candidates at Conservative Party conferences tended towards blue suits, I went on stage to make my speech in bright red.

I started life as an actress when the top audition tip was 'If you want the part, look the part.' When speaking, presenting or being interviewed I still use that acting experience. After all, Margaret Thatcher often wore red and the theatrical delivery worked for Tony Blair.

The twenty-first century has definitely brought a more relaxed approach to business attire, with dress-down Friday extending in some businesses to dressdown every day.

A recent survey discovered that there was confusion about what to wear at work, among women as well as men. The poll for Great Western Hotels GB found that 47 per cent of British people were confused about how to dress at meetings and conferences. Men have it easier when it comes to office dress because women are more scrutinised, but 32 per cent arrived underdressed for meetings. In Europe, Italy leads the way in the business-style stakes. The hotel has employed image guru Karen Kay to provide tips for its customers.

My advice for those attending a conference would be even though you're away, remember that you are dressing for a work-related function. It's easy to fall into clothing complacency when away from your traditional workplace environment, but this is a prime opportunity for management to view the future potential of their staff.

If you have seminars and presentations during the day, wear businesslike attire and treat it as a 'working wardrobe'. If your boss has told you that more informal clothes are acceptable, err on the side of caution. For example, I would suggest jeans are risky; opt for less casual skirts and trousers instead. Remember, you still need to make the effort to look presentable, even though you are dressed more casually, so make sure clothes are pressed neatly, shoes are polished and your hair is tidy.

In the early days of my career I was desperate to blend in rather than stand out. If I could have cloned the look of my successful peers, I would gladly have done just that. Remember this was the eighties, the *Dallas* and *Dynasty* years hotly followed on television by *LA Law*, all of which featured glamorous and beautifully attired women. I wanted to be like them with their designer outfits and beautiful jewellery. Challenging indeed on my limited income and without a retinue of stylists. The impossibility of it all didn't stop me trying.

I am certainly not beautiful, but always wanted to be glamorous. I wouldn't dream of going out of the house let alone going to work without the full war paint firmly in place. So the look I chose to perpetuate was glamour. You may choose bohemian or casual or au naturel, but I recommend that you choose. It is not a sin to look your best. It does not downgrade your professional skills. It will not make people think you can't do the job.

Wardrobe Malfunctions

I have had my share of Judy Finnegan moments. Remember Judy Finnegan when she inadvertently bared her bra to the nation after she and husband Richard Madeley collected an award for the most popular daytime TV programme at the 2000 National Television Awards? Her wardrobe malfunction has earned her a place in many 'worst moment' countdowns compiled since. Well, following a successful client meeting held in London in 2007 seven of us decided to enjoy a celebration dinner at a top restaurant. After waiting for me in the foyer while I went to the loo, we set off, six chaps and me, snaking in single file down Piccadilly among a throng of shoppers and sightseers. Only when I visited the toilet for a second time did I realise that my skirt had been tucked in my knickers throughout the journey. As several of the group I was with had followed me crocodile fashion they must have seen this fairly shocking sight but didn't say a word. Of course, when I returned to the table I pretended nothing had happened. Thank goodness it's not just me. Justine Dignam told me that once she was travelling by train, first class, with three business-men, all extremely serious. She reached up to pull her laptop from an overnight bag on the luggage rack and a pair of knickers came with it and fell like a dying bird on to the table between them. No one said a word as she scrabbled to retrieve them and stow them back above.

Wardrobe Faux Pas

But there are other kinds of wardrobe disasters that have haunted me in my working life, the sort only a woman can make. And these are really no laughing matter.

Not long ago I was working in Northern Ireland with a large and very successful company. I had been engaged to help them sell their business and had therefore met the executives on several occasions as we prepared the marketing information. All these meetings had taken place off-site to preserve confidentiality. However, it became essential that I visited their premises located in a very small rural community. I had chosen to wear a crossover black linen suit, knee length, but the crossover nature meant it showed a certain amount of leg whenever I walked or sat down. Being rather well endowed, I wore a scoop-neck T-shirt (conservative for me) rather than anything more plunging.

The meeting, including a tour of the premises, went well and I returned home thinking no more of it than any other assignment. However, the call I took the following day left me reeling. It was a complaint about my 'unsuitable' outfit from an intermediary who said that my revealing T-shirt (I promise you, for it to be revealing you needed a lot of imagination) and my skirt were not considered suitable business attire.

I have to say I genuinely thought it was some kind of wind-up. It wasn't and it was my mistake because I had not been as sensitive to their requirements as perhaps I should have been. To my mind I hadn't been outrageous or even overtly different, but the client wasn't happy with what I wore. Since then I have been careful to consider this. My own sense of personal fashion must be weighted against the client's propriety. Of course I could have been bloody-minded and just carried on, but to what avail? No, far better to take such matters on board and respond appropriately, out of courtesy.

In other words, daring to be different is one thing, offending others is something else. The former I approve of, the latter I do not. It's a view echoed by other women in the boardroom.

What to Wear and What Not to Wear

The Conservative Approach

Different career paths dictate varying standards of dress. The traditional professional roles – accountant, lawyer, etc. – tend to wear darker, more sober suits, while an IT or sports professional may go for more casual garb.

Deborah Adshead is the joint managing director of JD Approach, an IT company, operating in a field where women are rare. She is in no doubt that flamboyant dress is not the right route: 'Because you want to be taken seriously you need to look the part. Conform, because it helps you become accepted. As a woman in this industry I already stand out and that's enough.' Working in the same industry, another contributor and company owner who chose to remain anonymous uses the same low-key wardrobe approach:

> I'm all for being yourself and bringing your personality to work with you. I can't be anything but myself and, as a woman working in IT, I automatically stand out among my peers – which on the whole has been an advantage. However, there is a dress code in business in the UK and to disrespect it could damage your company's reputation. There are boundaries. Don't cross them.

As chief executive officer of the Institute of Mechanical Engineers Ruth Spellman is also a woman at large in a mostly male environment. Perhaps it is no surprise that she admits to being conventional: 'I do use colour, but I wear a suit. It's easy and suits me. I think you are judged by what you look like.'

Colour Counts

It is said that different colours say different things. Blue indicates intelligence, black power, red adventurousness – perhaps that's why my favourite colour is red! And I'm not alone in loving the power of scarlet, perhaps overused by ambitious women executives in the eighties but nonetheless still a statement today.

Fiona Sheridan, a partner in one of the country's top accountancy firms, has adopted more formal clothing since her promotion. Still, she says, 'I do use colour and like red jackets and suits that stand out.' Red is also a tool used by Gail Carter, the owner of a business management company. 'I dress smartly, wear colour, avoid boring suits and use scarves. I wear red lipstick if I want to be powerful.' Tracy Viner thinks that 'You need to mirror your audience – but I try to avoid black. Colour makes me stand out.'

Accessorise

A plain suit can be made to dazzle by a bright accessory. When dress codes are rigid accessories are the device to make you stand out in a crowd.

Denise Collins, group HR director of 3i, admits to being old-fashioned when it comes to wardrobe: 'It helps me enormously to look smart. I always wear a business suit as it gives me presence and confidence. But I don't want to look dull and boring, so I wear classic clothes with an accessory. I'm also conscious of the code of business black-tie dinners. It's not appropriate to have acres of flesh on show.'

Jeanette Sargent runs a jewellery company so not surprisingly she has the following advice: 'Wear a distinctive piece of jewellery as it can initiate conversation and you may be remembered for it. It can also make you feel good. I always wear a contemporary but stylish necklace at business meetings.' As for clothes, she tends to stick to one style-conscious chain store that produces clothes and colours she feels comfortable wearing. She never wears a plunging neckline, nor does she opt for a suit. 'Views on womenswear in the boardroom vary widely and it depends whether you want to blend in or make a statement. You must assess how any statement made through clothes will impact on your target audience.'

'I think it's fundamental to dress properly but to retain femininity. I love accessories, grooming is critical and I have a signature style. I love shoes and big beads and people recognise me for that,' says Natalie Douglas of IDIS Limited, and Fiona Cruickshank of the Specials Laboratory Limited admits to struggling in achieving her aim of looking well groomed. Nonetheless, she chooses never to fall back on those old chestnuts of opting for black or a suit. 'Here's a hot tip from an artistic friend and colleague of mine – wear pointy boots. Men are scared of them!'

A Cut Above

If in doubt, splash out. Top of the range designer clothes make a statement about you that leaves observers in no doubt about your readiness for the task in hand. When she worked for a large agency, Nicky Pattinson discovered people made judgements about her after hearing a broad Yorkshire accent. 'After speaking to me over the phone clients had a perception about what I looked like. [When I met them] I could see it in their faces. They thought I would be two feet six inches tall and nineteen stone.' In fact, with Italian heritage, she is a tall and attractive woman. And just to nail any doubts left by her colloquial use of English, she wears Prada suits and Gucci shoes.

Critical Eye

Women at work are on parade in a way men never are which is why it's important to understand what your clothes say about you. Nicola

Kay, CEO, MD and major shareholder in an electronic component manufacturing and distribution company, believes dress code to be critical. 'Staff notice the slightest change – although they don't in men. I have learned to always dress well and try to look good even when I don't feel good.' Another woman who has been unfairly scrutinised on her clothing is TV presenter Clare Balding. 'At Ascot they criticised me on dress. They wouldn't do this with a man.'

Other Tips

With clothes, as with life, there is a middle path that's a clever mix of conformity and individuality. Kate Ancketill has some tips about dress code, learned the hard way:

Never wear a short skirt. They will never take you seriously as a CEO. I also learned that if you show any cleavage you don't get the job. Previously I'd always felt that if you've got it, flaunt it. But in my experience if you wear anything slightly see-through or fruity you don't sell the service. The men in the room are just looking at your knockers. So in the end I did have to care about what I wore.

I am British, although most of my work is in the US. But that allows me to be more quirky. I wear Vivien Westwood and red boots, which is my brand. And, as I am usually the only female, I stand out and everyone remembers me. Ninety per cent of a presentation is about you.

Diana Green believes it is important to stand out in a crowd. 'I try not to be a woman in men's clothes,' she explains. 'I take care with what I wear, buying good-quality clothes, and keep my hair immaculate as well.' For Alison Boxall, the creator of Izziwizzikids, the message is simple: 'Be yourself,' she says, 'reflect your business and you.' Fiona

Vanstone, a chairman's PA and office manager, believes making an effort with your appearance can be crucial. 'Have a good mix-and-match wardrobe,' she advises. 'Nothing too sexy, too short or that exposes too much cleavage. Be well groomed as taking care of your appearance indicates you will take care with your work.'

Of course, success in the boardroom is not just down to sassy clothing. As Pooya Ahmadi notes: 'Brush up your magic and beauty, be yourself and believe in yourself. You have nothing to prove except that you want to do business.'

Appearances Count

Coco Chanel's statement probably says it much better than I could ever do. I suppose it's not so much daring to be different that counts, but looking immaculate that really matters. But, I hear you say, looks don't matter as long as you get the job done. Smart suits and styled hair amount to nothing more than superficial eye candy, so why bother?

Of course getting the job done does come first and foremost but your chances of doing the job in the first place may be substantially reduced if you don't get the look right. Recent statistics have shown that active discrimination exists in abundance for those of us who carry more pounds than are desirable. You will be only too familiar with the commonly held notion that interview decisions are made within the first few minutes of meeting. Therefore, a large proportion of that decision must inevitably be based on appearance.

Whatever attire I have chosen – and some outfits I freely admit have been inappropriate – I have never tried to hide my femininity. I love being a woman and I like to celebrate that. My husband is forever asking me why I wear such high heels, particularly as I have a tendency to fall off them! Last year I did so when I was running for a train and managed to break my foot. Not only was my right leg in plaster for six weeks but, to my absolute horror, I couldn't immediately go back into my stilettos and had to wear flat pumps for a further three months until I regained the strength in my ankle. I hated every minute of it. I guess I'm not a flat pumps sort of girl. If you are a high-heeled shoe wearer, you will understand what I mean. That's the style that suits me.

Now it's time to assess the style for you. Most people have adopted a trademark look before their twenties have expired. Could it be that it's time to move on from the skirts and shirts that you've worn for years? With comfort comes confidence, so there's no need to be unduly radical. Most people stick with what they know for fear of making mistakes.

BUSINESS-WEAR SURVIVAL GUIDE

■ Your height and relative size obviously affect your choice of clothes. I am a national average – a 14 to 16 and 5 feet 4 inches – so forget skinny jeans and mini dresses while the new-look smock tops make me look six months pregnant. Maturity and success have given me the sense not to follow fashion and the funds to afford better-fitting clothes. This hasn't always been the case; as I have said, I have made more than a few mistakes – who hasn't!

- As you know, high heels are my personal choice, but when it comes to footwear don't sacrifice comfort for style. It's worth taking an extra hour in the shopping centre looking for the right shoes that look and feel the part rather than condemning yourself to hobbling between meetings for the foreseeable future.

- Recently I discovered personal shoppers – a free service available (by booking) at most large department stores. Although I generally know what suits me, this service has taken me out of my comfort zone and I love it.

- I have always invested in a good haircut every four weeks, along with a manicure and pedicure every six weeks. Yes, they are luxuries and you may not be in the position to afford them yet, but this has been my choice because they raise my spirits, as well as offering that essential 'me' time.

- Remember, dressing the part isn't only required within office hours, as more and more often we have to spend time outside the office entertaining or being entertained. Your look is just as important after 5.30. My own view on this is that less is more. Certainly when I was younger I turned up at too many events looking like the Christmas fairy! Fellow guests would have been forgiven for thinking a tin of Quality Street wrappers had exploded all over me. My children would say I still have 'magpie' tendencies, drawn as I am to anything remotely sparkly for such outings. By and large, I feel that it's always the people who dress with elegance who stand out.

■ When it's a black-tie event, always check if it is long or short dresses for women so you don't have to worry you're standing out from the crowd for the wrong reasons. I welcome the opportunity to wear long dresses. After all, the chances to haul them out of the wardrobe these days are very limited.

So, in summary, in daring to be different, then maybe I'm not so daring after all – what I dare to be is myself!

CHAPTER 5

Playing Games

I don't work out. If God had wanted us to bend over,
He would have put diamonds on the floor.
Joan Rivers, comedian

The first time I see a jogger smiling, I'll consider it.
Joan Rivers, comedian

How do you make networking work for you?

It's amazing what you can gain from people going through the same experiences as you. **Perween Warsi**

Ask people about themselves. **Sonita Alleyne**

Smile and have fun. **Justine Dignam**

Smile, look into people's eyes and be brave, even in a room full of strangers. **Nicola Kay**

Use humour to make people feel at ease. **Deirdre Bounds**

Be genuine, connect with people. **Julia Moir**

Be genuinely interested in people. If not, it shows. Get out and share. You always get more back than you put in. **Christina Vaughan**

Don't sell, be interested, find common ground and leave your new-found companion with an interesting piece of information about you. **Fay Sharpe**

Leave the door open for future meetings. **Alison Kennedy**

Be short, sweet and to the point. **Anita Brough**

When it comes to networking people either love it or loathe it. But, whether we like it or not, it is an increasingly vital aspect of modern business.

Often the glad-handing and small talk has given way to some major sporting activity that has team building and communication somewhere near its heart. And if connections and networking are part of the critical path to success this path is often littered with balls of various sizes and colours. Beloved by senior executives who are otherwise office bound, this sporting life doesn't suit everyone. Especially me. Of course lots of women love sports but many don't and a great number wish to watch rather than participate.

This section deals with what's essential and what's desirable and if, like me, the thought of any sort of sport is an abomination, how to deal with this dilemma.

Game On

At school we had games every Wednesday afternoon – lacrosse in winter and netball in summer – without exception. And every Wednesday I managed to have a nose bleed brought on by a sharp poke administered from my forefinger – before class started of course! Sometimes to my dismay these bloody interludes were only short-lived and our enthusiastic games teacher would still drag me onto whatever field or court the activity was taking place upon. Humiliatingly, I was always the last to be picked for a team: that awful process of everybody else's name being shouted out by the captains until I stood alone on the sidelines is unforgettable.

Basically I hated everything about sport – the cold (or the heat), the exhaustion, the shapeless tops, those awful games knickers! Big blue baggy ones and, later, those very unflattering grey polyester culottes – yuk! On top of that at Waverley Girls School my house was Kennelworth and our home colour a dull flat pea green. Maybe I'd have played better if I'd been in Melrose whose home colour was a sunny yellow – but then again I seriously doubt it! There were always those sporty girls in whatever house who seemed to thrive on these games and even – God forbid – volunteer for extra sporting activities including tennis and gymnastics. I just didn't get it.

My husband, an avid Arsenal fan, persists in detailing matches and results after fifteen years of me telling him I don't give a flying fig. My brother-in-law goes shooting, even more dire than regular sport as part of this activity requires you to handle various dead birds. And as for golf . . . please tell me how knocking a small white ball round fields and valleys can be enjoyed by anyone.

Clearly my view is not universally held. Take Executive Dean of Sheffield Hallam University Christine Booth, for example, who is committed to exercise – and for very good reasons: 'I have a routine and I make time for exercise. I cycle, run and teach yoga. Exercise gets rid of stress and keeps me sane,' she told me. Fair enough, but I have a theory that a lot of people just pretend to enjoy these things for the sake of business rewards dangled at the finishing line.

The problem is that these sporting activities are often favoured by men and, although I don't subscribe to the theory that deals are done on the golf course, I am absolutely certain that vital contacts are made there, allowing deals to be done at a later stage. I admit it is inevitable that bonds, social and professional, are created in these various arenas, be it via the camaraderie of the team spirit or indeed the sheer number of man hours spent together trawling around the eighteen holes on the golf course. I am certain, and always have been, that business is done with people you tend to like, and time spent pursuing various sporting activities does, it seems, give space to form friendships – ones that may even last a lifetime.

Participate

Having recognised that this sporting arena can create business opportunities, some years ago I threw caution to the wind and booked myself a dozen golf lessons. I turned up promptly for the first lesson. I was not exactly looking forward to it but I had a sense of purpose and, well, how hard could it be? Bored, boring, oh my word, who cared whether my hands should be placed over each other, further up, round or down the bloody stick. Certainly not me. After twenty minutes I was counting the seconds until I was dismissed.

But I'm not one to give up easily, particularly when I have paid up in advance. I stoically turned up for the next few sessions, albeit later and later until I accepted that, realistically, I was never going to enjoy this, so what was the point. I wrote the rest of the classes off as a business expense and vowed never to repeat such an exercise.

In truth, golf is loved by many women. I am simply not one of them. My dilemma was what other activity I might tolerate. (I am avoiding the word 'enjoy' as I cannot in all honesty put sport and enjoyment together in the same sentence.) A colleague suggested joining a gym. I'd done this before and always started off very enthusiastically, but after the first few mind-numbingly dull sessions of pounding a tread-mill, going nowhere, I found every excuse not to go. Besides which, the £700-a-year membership fee worked out for me to approximately £100 a session, so it would probably have been cheaper to build my own gymnasium and kit it out. Anyway, as far as enhancing business links the gym is pretty much a non-starter. It really isn't possible to form business relationships at a time when it's barely possible to draw breath, let alone speak!

I considered tennis but – well, it's all so seasonal, what would I do in the winter? (I ignored the indoor court suggestion – that's not real tennis is it? And I'm nothing if not a purist.) Squash is too fast, clay pigeon shooting too loud. Ladies football? I think not. Clearly sport and me were not meant to be.

Basically, I'm far better at spectating than I am at participating.

Spectating

As most of my clients over the years have been male and, as entertaining in corporate finance fields is considered a given, I have been compelled to place sport high on the agenda. Consequently, I have been forced to identify suitable pastimes that allow me to have a reasonably pleasant time, in what is generally considered an acceptable sporting arena.

For me horse racing has proved the most suitable medium, providing the opportunity for a flutter at whatever level you and your clients wish to participate, while allowing myself and any other female clients the opportunity to dress up for the occasion, which might also extend to sitting about sipping champagne and chatting. I am told that appropriate county cricket events and even tennis championships provide the same ambiance, though in my opinion there is less opportunity for just milling around. Secretly I admit this is more akin to corporate entertaining than participating in a sporting activity, but I do feel I am making at least some concession.

Despite my genuine and deep-rooted hate of all things sporty I can still talk with low-grade knowledge about nationally significant football matches. It does help having a football-crazy husband and stepson; it means I cannot escape from immersion in the Premier League for at least half the year. Some of it, I'm sure, I absorb through osmosis. At any rate, when it comes to talking with clients I don't know well, this can sometimes provide some (short-lived) common ground. And it's true that sometimes misguided potential customers might leave with the impression I am a soccer-mad, rugby-watching cricket hag.

While I don't advocate lying about your interest in whatever sporting activity your client or potential client enjoys, genning up on the game will do you no harm, and it can act as a vital ice-breaker in conversation. Obviously it's advisable not to look too keen, though, in case you might, God forbid, be invited to join in or watch some ghastly muddy event as your client/professional relationship develops.

What works for me is recounting the enthusiasm of my nearest and dearest as a conversation model. It works even if the client is a Manchester United fan against my other half's passion for Arsenal, for no other reason than the derogatory comments that spew forth.

Delegate

Thankfully, as I have reached a more senior role, I now have the option of sending/encouraging members of my team to pick up the sports baton. By and large the younger members, particularly the males, seem to participate willingly in said activities week in, week out, and who am I to persuade them otherwise? As a firm we have done everything from weekly five-a-side, inter-professional matches to fantasy football leagues. My own position remaining that of 'ideas' person, I have even been known to go to the awards or prize-giving ceremony if I am pushed, and being the 'face' of such activities does keep you in the frame. All I ask is to be left alone when it comes to picking the teams.

Networking

For all my criticism and a natural abhorrence for sporting commitments I concede that it is an ideal way to start networking. This is the one aspect of business life that has assumed huge importance in the past few years and remains a stumbling block for many.

Who you know often counts as much as what you know. Your professional and social networks – which often overlap – are built up over a lifetime and if used correctly are invaluable in helping you climb up, and stay at the top of, the professional ladder.

My own extensive network has helped me secure new positions, create sales opportunities and open otherwise firmly closed doors.

Endure It

Unlike many of my peers, I am not a naturally sociable person. I have to work very hard to get to the numerous events I am invited to. I absolutely dread going to some do or other where I will not know anyone, and invariably will be the only woman or, at best, one of just a few. If you have ever had that awful sinking feeling as you enter yet another bland function room and are presented with a glass of disgusting warm white wine, you will know what I mean.

Steeling yourself for such functions is, however, essential if you want to build your network. I go through a positive process of psyching myself up before I enter the designated arena, much in the way I imagine Daniel did before entering the lion's den. For years I have believed myself to be a social freak for having such reluctance. It was with a sense of relief I realised that, virtually without exception, my interviewees echoed my trepidation and dread with regard to these particular activities.

How do you get through networking events?

There are different ways to tackle the dilemma presented by networking. I'm going to hand you over to the contributors who have added extra dimensions to this book to find out more.

Natalie Douglas 'I walk into rooms and am terrified. But I smile – it's bloody hard but it works. And I target the first person I see not talking to someone.'

Denise Collins 'I am not good at this. I don't like it when I don't know people. I hate striking up conversation with people I haven't met before. I resent the cut into my own personal time for evening events and I don't find people well mannered. My advice is to have a thick skin.'

Anne Lockwood 'Networking is the one area I dislike. I find it difficult to break into a group of people who are clearly having a discussion. I dislike that feeling of standing on the edge, smiling like a Cheshire cat waiting for your turn to speak – and then all eyes are on you when you do say something. My top networking technique is – send someone else to do it.'

Ann Worrall 'Take an interest – a real one – in the person you are talking to, trust yourself and don't get worked up.'

Sue Catling, a prospective parliamentary candidate, has spent many evenings networking in order to improve her chances at the polls. In doing so she has learned one valuable lesson. 'Many of the people you meet on occasions like this are bar flies. A great deal of networking takes place late at night and is fuelled by alcohol. Have one glass of wine to appear sociable. Then keep topping up your glass with water. No one will know you're not drinking and when all around you are becoming ever more indiscreet, you'll be in a fit state to capitalise on what you've heard.'

If you are still shaking in your boots, think outside the box and ponder if there are other ways around the problem. Barbara Scandrett, for example, suggests a lecture that can be prepared and practised before the big day.

Enjoy It

No matter how negatively you view networking it's important to treat it just as you would any other business meeting. Be professional, have targets, set goals . . . and smile. If you practise hard enough, you might even get to enjoy events that once had you running for the hills.

Anon

I treat networking as a social event and as such aim to enjoy myself as much as I can. Be friendly and don't push your business on people.

Don't expect to come away with orders. People need time to get to know you and trust you, so if there's someone whose business you really want, aim to attend a few of the same events and ensure you end up in conversation. If that person has not asked to find out more about what you do by the third occasion, bite the bullet and request a meeting.

Work the Room

On how many occasions are important contacts gathered in one place, at one time? Usually, only at the best networking events. It's time to make hay for your business and that means working the room, leaving no potential contact without face time. Julia Gash, another woman with political experience and founder of her own company, gives this advice:

Work the room. As soon as you enter make a mental note of all the people you want to connect with. It's your mission to get to speak to all of them and say whatever it is you need to let them know. Conversations therefore have to be kept to a certain length of time but you have to be polite, positive, charming and unhurried at all times – and never pushy. You then introduce the person you're in conversation with to someone else, which enables you to move on as you're not abandoning them.

Be Interested

The art of being interested is easy to develop. Just ensure the conversation is not about you but about the person facing you. Usually, you will become so absorbed you won't notice how time slips by and an evening you dreaded has passed pleasantly and maybe even profitably.

Sarah Deaves, chief executive of Coutts & Co, has a genuine interest in people. Everyone has a passion and she regards it her duty to discover what makes her companion of the moment tick. 'Usually I start with questions about home, family, likes and dislikes and the conversation flows. Then you can get down to business much more effectively.'

Helen Merfield is empathetic to others at networking events. 'It's easy to feel like a lemon. Look for someone on their own and bring them into your circle. It helps them relax and broadens the group. And those individuals will remember what you did for them.' However, she warns, you can ruin all this good groundwork if you start trying to sell at all costs and, as Pinky Lilani, founder of Spice Magic, points out, it's not about you but about them.

Set Targets

Just as you set targets every day at work so you must make them for networking events, if you are to come away with something positive.

Jeanette Sargent, who owns her own business, is a target-setter. 'Aim to talk to at least six strangers and maybe end up having coffee with one or two. Listen to the other person, don't just appear to. People who feel compelled to work the whole room may come across as shallow.' Yvonne Lumley, of Leading Women, suggests being brutally focused at networking events. 'Don't stick with business-only groups or women-only groups. Eighty per cent of the people you meet won't be of any value to you.'

Conversation Pieces

Once you've exhausted conversation about the person you've just met it can be a challenge to find fresh topics. Having some sound bites up your sleeve may not be enough, so keep abreast of current events or other subjects you know well and can talk about with ease.

'Be informed and know your subject well. Speak with passion and enthusiasm and don't patronise. Above all, be fun,' suggests Hannah Evans, founder of Piccalilly, while Wendy Duckham, a sales and marketing director, has a networking formula that she finds successful: 'Understand that everyone is probably shy so make a move, be inclusive, smile and tell stories they will remember you for.' For Linda Hinxman, the key is getting off the predictable topics of business and sport and engaging on a personal level.

Take Note

It helps to have an elephantine memory in which to log personal details for months or years to come. If memory lapses are a problem, consider a detailed contacts database so you can add birthdays, holidays, spouse's names and so forth. Fiona Vanstone, of AMEC plc, points out: 'People are impressed if you can remember some personal details as well as business details.' Tracy Viner makes notes on the back of the business cards she receives before adding them to her contacts list: 'Networking is what makes me succeed,' she admits. 'Following up is essential.'

Follow-ups

Having put in the time at a networking event, don't let the effort made go to waste by failing to install a newly made contact in your address book. It's just one of several bits of wisdom that contributors imparted to help you make the most of networking events. Don't forget to follow up a meeting with an email, a call or a visit, says one contributor. Send out catalogues or product samples where appropriate.

'Be generous with the contact you make and you get it back tenfold,' says Alexis Cleveland, and head of Cabinet Office Management,

'I often send out "please help" emails and generally expect a good response.'

Nicole Paradise is choosy about the networking events she attends. And her golden rule? 'Don't get drunk. Don't make a fool of yourself. For while men can get away with this, women can't.' Fiona Cruickshank suggests a positive attitude and a desire to learn. It's a sure way to make the most of the day.

So it would seem that most women don't really enjoy enforced networking but have all accepted it as a necessary evil. It does make you wonder why we can't somehow make socialising more appealing, and begs the question – do men feel the same?

I have not researched into this, so can only make suppositions based on my experience. My male colleagues seem more at home at these events. Maybe it's just because there are more of them? Or maybe (and I realise this is controversial) they are concentrating on the task in hand and not concerning themselves with getting home and making supper, doing the shopping, putting the children to bed, doing the ironing, etc. Men also seem to be able to bond more easily over a few pints at these events than my female peers – sipping their one glass of warm Chardonnay.

Of course, these professional networking events are not the sole arena upon which to build your web, but if we agree they're a 'must do' then I have some tips on making the most of them.

NETWORKING SURVIVAL GUIDE

■ Smile: it's the quickest way to break down barriers – don't forget, many people will be feeling as you are and a friendly smile helps put people at their ease.

■ If you know no one at all, don't hang round the edges of the room like the proverbial wallflower. You are not at the school disco waiting for the spotty oik to ask you to dance – you need to be proactive. Take a deep breath and approach either another sole delegate or a small group. Be honest – the approach I take is: 'Hi there, look I don't know anyone here, would you mind if I join you?' Very few people (it has never happened to me) will reject you.

■ Don't launch into a big sales speech! This is deadly, and deadly boring! It may be advisable to use a simple ice-breaker – if it's in your personality, a bit of humour helps – something like, 'I see it's vintage wine they are serving again!'

■ Ask open questions. Most people like to talk about themselves; remember this is your opportunity to find out about this person and ascertain whether they should be in your network.

■ Be empathetic: particularly with another woman. Find common ground, it helps with the bonding process.

■ Be genuine: I can spot false interest a mile off – I'm not alone, don't be sycophantic.

■ Do share contact information. If this turns out to be a genuine networking opportunity – make sure you swap business cards, preferably as you part – do not thrust your card on to someone the moment you meet them.

■ If the person is a total bore, or you need to move on to meet others, be polite and tactful. My techniques vary regarding this. If you don't know anyone else, I would usually be honest and say how nice it has been to meet them, then I would try 'Excuse me, I want to circulate a bit', or use the loo, get another drink, whatever lever you think most appropriate.

■ Set yourself targets: as one interviewee suggested, if you have an hour at one of these events, set a personal goal of meeting six new people – if half an hour – three new people, etc. I loved the idea and intend to try it at my next event – if nothing else it makes it more of a game.

■ If you really want to be successful, go to these events alone. It makes you be more sociable; if you go with a colleague it's just too easy to stick together, a bit pointless really.

■ Follow up. If you have promised to contact someone, do so and do it quickly – by email, phone or letter as appropriate.

> ■ Send thank you notes. Remember that a huge amount of effort
> goes into these events, even if you haven't particularly enjoyed
> it – you went. A well-penned personal note (handwritten is
> a lovely touch) will mean you will be remembered for your
> thoughtfulness.

Alternatives

These professional events are of course only one way of building your network (any number of alternatives are available). My experience is that people generally work with those they like. That doesn't mean being best buddies, but it does mean you have to get on, build trust and respect.

If you are of the sporty persuasion, club membership and participation will almost certainly bring rewards. As I am not this way inclined I have had to find alternatives.

Events

As a professional speaker firmly established on the national circuit, I meet hundreds, if not thousands of people each year. As I am often privileged to be the key-note speaker, speaking for a fraction of an hour or over a number of days, this has given me a fabulous opportunity to build my network because, inevitably, you can build rapport and trust amazingly quickly on public-speaking occasions.

What I have found quite gratifying is that I make contacts at the events, and not only do they often give me an exclusive opportunity such as a sales lead, but very often people approach me months, and even years, after an initial meeting.

I inevitably swap business cards and make sure they are put on my database, so when I do any mail shot or PR activity, they are automatically included as a tame audience, so to speak.

Referrals

Referrals probably create some of your best networks, being extra-special by virtue of the fact that a trusted, commonly known party has made the introduction. Such activities work even better on a tit-for-tat basis, so make sure you reciprocate if relevant.

Internet

And of course the internet has created a fantastic networking forum with sites both social and professional, dedicated to such opportunities. A colleague recently introduced me to a fabulous website – www.linkedin.com which allows you to download critical details about yourself, your personal services, references, etc. and build a three-dimensional worldwide reference and contact forum. (See Resources on page 219 for more information.)

Classes and Clubs

The other route is, of course, to think outside the business box. Sports clubs we have already mentioned, but I have made contacts at evening classes and charity events. Although I am not a member of many clubs myself, I am certain that business relationships flourish as a result of membership of Rotary and Round Table, let alone the Masons (and there are women's versions).

Maintaining Your Contacts

So, having built networks, the key point is of course to maintain them.

Before technology was so sophisticated, I kept my contacts on an old-fashioned Rolodex, absolutely horrendous to manage, but at least I had a permanent alphabetical list. Now of course I store the data on my computer and BlackBerry, and can split it into professional sectors and so on. Great for proactive contacts when required.

One interviewee told me a wonderful story about how when she was travelling and had time to kill, she would send an email to fifty or so people in her address book as follows: 'Sorry we haven't spoken in a while, was just thinking of you and wondering how you were doing. Give me a ring when you have a moment.' On average, she got back ten or so messages, and often resurrected a relationship that led to sales opportunities.

Rapid advances in new technology does mean that keeping contact is a whole lot easier than it once was. Don't turn your nose up at social networking sites either. Like it or not, Facebook, MySpace and the rest are here to stay and will play their part increasingly in modern business life. If you want to know what's hot and what's not, check out what's happening on those highly connected sites – or ask a teenager!

The prospect of including your own profile on just such a site might send shudders down your spine, but you can bet you will be doing it within a few years in order to make the most of this valuable networking tool. While some big corporations have placed a ban on access to Facebook, Deloitte is one company far-sighted enough to embrace it and employees are encouraged to include their profile on it, without being too personal. Tom Crawford, Deloitte's head of diversity, told *The Times* on 3 October 2007: 'The great thing about Facebook internally is that it's a great social leveller. Members of the board are on there as well as people who have just joined the firm.' Already the company uses internal blogs to inspire dialogue. The next step for Deloitte is to use dedicated spaces on its computers for teams to keep in touch.

Whether you like this or not, contact is important. At the last count I had over 3,000 contacts on my network database – impossible of course to keep in touch with all of them and inevitably some will have moved on. But if you don't maintain some sort of contact, all that hard work building it is pretty useless.

I have found it quite helpful to label contacts into groups, such as:

- professional by sector

- clients

- active

- dormant

- potential

As and when I can, I mail them with something of relevance – a basic marketing technique really. It's all about reminding them you are there.

As well as doing business with people we like, there is sometimes an inclination to do business with the latest person you've met and liked so it's important to make sure you are in the top tier of contacts.

My final tip would be never underestimate the potential of a contact. By and large I will speak to most people, or even meet them. I don't advocate the use of the dragon at the door secretary approach. I have made some very successful deals with contacts I have thought on initial meeting would not bring any sort of fruitful results.

Of course time is always an issue but just bear this in mind!

CHAPTER 6

Education, Education, Education

Nothing is a waste of time if you use the experience wisely.
Auguste Rodin, sculptor

*If you can't be a good example – then you'll just have to be
a horrible warning.*
Anon

What qualification do you wish you had?

I don't regret not going to university but I wish that sometimes I had more patience and was a better listener. **Rosemary Conley**

Qualifications are important, but I don't believe they are everything. People who are enthusiastic, have drive and are keen to learn should have just as much opportunity as those with formal qualifications. **Perween Warsi**

A coaching qualification, very useful in business. **Julia Moir**

A much better understanding of accounts would be very helpful. **Rolline Frewen**

The best qualification really does come from the university of life. **Christina Vaughan**

I wish I was more able in coaching and mentoring. **Alexis Cleveland**

A degree – any degree. **Gail Carter**

Experience is far more valuable and rewarding than qualifications. **Hannah Evans**

There's no need for education to stop when you leave school or college. It's neither necessary nor desirable for that to happen. Education is a broad church that includes academic qualifications, self-development, spiritual enlightenment and a whole range of other skills. There's something out there even for school phobics, like myself. It took me some time to realise the joy of learning and I know from the investigations I've done with other businesswomen that I am not alone in that.

No matter how dreary your school days were, it's time to overcome those old prejudices and stick your hand up when the chance for training, development and qualifications come your way. Courses may not send you straight to the top of the corporate ladder but rarely is a spell of further education entirely wasted. Perhaps more crucially, this section will deal with what is a must, where to find it and how to fund it.

The Pursuit of Knowledge

I hated school and was hopeless at most subjects, except house-craft (cooking and sewing for those readers under the age of forty!), I couldn't spell and was later to discover I was dyslexic. As far as algebra and geometry were concerned, I couldn't tell one from the other, and as for languages, well, it was only French at my school but, for me, the choice between a French class and a half marathon would have been a close-run thing.

However, when I went to our local technical college the winds of change breezed through my hitherto unremarkable academic life. I had failed my eleven-plus and it was either the tech or the local secondary modern. I chose the former. This was the early 1970s, and the choice of courses for girls was comparatively limited. They did offer science subjects but it was assumed a girl would never make that choice and, of course, I didn't.

What the tech did offer me, however, was a much wider choice of O levels. I have no idea why, but one of my choices was law. There were no lawyers in my family – but there had been some compelling legal dramas on TV, so maybe that's what pushed me in this particular direction. In any event, it was the subject – or perhaps more the teacher – that lured me away from the bottom of the class. I went from being very uninterested in my approach to being someone who was super keen on a school subject. This early introduction to the law was the inspiration that motivated me to make a career in which legal knowledge plays an important role.

I have alluded here to the quality of the teaching at the tech and it was this that proved as important as the subject, if not more so. My law teacher was inspiring, entertaining, funny and simply wonderful. He made a potentially drab subject captivating, filling me with a desire to find out more. Eventually I took a degree in law.

Once I discovered the joy of learning it was unshakeable. My own personal quest for training and development was insatiable from that moment on.

The Joy of Learning

Not everyone is a qualifications fiend. Anne Lockwood of First Choice Select Limited admits that 'I'm not that big on qualifications. I got a smattering of O levels and then achieved a degree in savvy. That's defined as quick, clever, acute, alert, astute, deft, responsive, sharp, smart, wise, knowing, perceptive, receptive and feminine!'

But there's much more to education than the formal, mortar-board variety that initially springs to mind. Sometimes I take courses just for the pleasure of learning, often going completely 'off-piste'. That's why I am a qualified aromatherapist and hypnotherapist. Yes, really! I'd like to think hypnotherapy at least has a place in the world of corporate finance. And of course I now spend a considerable amount of my time training others in anything from being a director to buying and selling businesses. If I am honest, even when I am the trainer I am being trained myself. I always learn something from my audience, be it a different legal point or a point of view. Crucially, I am always learning and developing.

The trick is not to see training as a chore, but rather as a joy; not a must have, mandatory requirement but a want to have in the sense of a real desire.

Some of the training I have undergone has been paid for by previous employers. That includes computer programming – yes, I did that and hated it, but I did it – to financial services updates. I didn't enjoy those much either, to be honest, although neither were entirely wasted. In addition, there have been numerous courses that I have funded myself over the years – just because I wanted to.

If you have a professional qualification, some sort of continuous professional development (CPD) is required to maintain your accreditation and clearly there are must haves – although you may have a choice of what these might include. Be broad in your choice rather than sticking to the safe option. Usually there aren't any exams to worry about so the pressure you might have had in relation to demonstrating a technical competence is not there. You can use the opportunity to immerse yourself in a subject for the simple pleasure of becoming an armchair expert.

And, anyway, why restrict training to the essentials if time and funds permit otherwise? Why not explore other personal development opportunities? What have you got to lose?

Many of us – including me – have experienced a career crisis. Mine came at forty – sorry to be so predictable, but it did. The training and development I had undertaken helped me find my way out of that particular dilemma and the more training I did over that period the clearer-sighted I became. Finally the confusion that had enveloped me vanished without trace. As it happened, the right way was back to where I had been before, but that's not really relevant. It was the insight gained via the training I had done that illustrated to me that I was in the right career!

Learning for Career Progression

The question is, does training per se help your career? Does it help your promotion prospects? Despite what I've just said and done myself, my honest opinion is that I don't think it does, or at least not on its own. There are clearly countless examples of men and women who made good with little or no formal education, let alone degrees or professional qualifications, so it must go without saying that the accreditation process itself will not move you through the ranks.

Some formal qualifications are clearly necessary for certain career paths. You can't be a chartered accountant unless you have passed the relevant exams. The same goes for a solicitor, a vet or a doctor. Technical qualifications are necessary, so you make sure you pass them, but passing alone does not guarantee you success in your chosen field – and certainly doesn't guarantee you promotion. If these are areas in which you wish to play, the basic qualifications are essential. It is those professions that don't have a must-have accreditation in which debate is worthwhile.

Many of the self-made women I interviewed had no more than a handful of O levels or GCSEs between them, yet still they have hugely successful careers. Some said they didn't want anything more formal than those few certificates gained years ago.

Angela Hughes, shareholder and commercial director of JVL Products, a £30-million-turnover importer says, 'I don't think I could do my job if I'd had any professional sales training, I know I don't work to the book but that's what makes me successful, in my view.'

Kate Ancketill, MD of GDR Creative Intelligence

I was a mall rat. There was no where else to go where I grew up and Brent Cross, the first British mall, was just down the road. My mum worked there, so I was there a lot. Ultimately I knew where everything was in every shop. It has been a useful experience.

I wish I had qualifications in good business practice, accounting and corporate governance but, as I can't be good at everything, I employ people to do it for me. I don't have a paper qualification. To be successful, most people make it up as they go along.

Government Initiatives

The government has invested massively over the last thirty years in training and development schemes for adults and work returners with Industry Training Boards, Training and Enterprise Councils and latterly Business Links, which provides advice on all aspects of company life. Hugely subsidised programmes have been introduced countrywide to encourage businesses to invest in the training of their staff. The vast funds available in the 1980s and 90s have been redirected but, clearly, there is still massive financial help available if you are prepared to source it.

Although a professional and a trainer myself I am always staggered by how little I actually know, especially about things not on my immediate horizon. I'm on a perpetual quest to discover what I didn't know I didn't know.

One of the very best training and development programmes I found was Common Purpose. Formed in 1989, it aims to offer insight to business leaders that will ultimately result in better working practice across the board. As its website explains: 'The problems that most need solving cross boundaries – and the way to solve them is to do the same. Leaders are most effective when they broaden their horizons and their networks. Real change doesn't just happen: leaders need to make it happen . . . Since 1989, more than 120,000 people have been involved in Common Purpose and 20,000 leaders from every area of the UK have completed one or more of our programmes.'

In practice this hugely successful national initiative brings together groups of around twenty to thirty people in their home town or region, from cross-functional disciplines for a twelve-month period. During this time you meet once a month to explore and share widely different experiences. Typically a group will consist of private sector representatives, such as myself, with public sector personnel from the police, NHS or local authority, for example, as well as representatives from charities and the voluntary sector.

This interactive training is fantastic, exposing you as it does to areas you are unlikely to encounter in your own field. I visited prisons, mental health establishments, all-girl Muslim schools and television studios during my year. It was some of the best personal development I have ever been involved in. It took me entirely out of my comfort zone and challenged my usual thought processes. Yes, the costs were a consideration: I paid for the course myself at a time when I could ill afford the £2,500 fee. But it was in terms of time and commitment that I felt the pinch. The one full day a month proved a mighty chunk out of my businesses, leaving a hole in my earnings and a backlog of work. What I didn't know then was that I could probably have got a grant for this. Nobody told me and I didn't bother to ask. Not following the advice of my motto 'If you don't ask you generally won't get' was a mistake.

What this experience did tell me was that training isn't about highly structured sessions in classrooms. Indeed, the best personal development processes I have been involved in have been anything but this.

After being a speaker for many years for organisations such as the Institute of Directors, Vistage, the world's largest CEO membership organisation, and the Academy of Chief Executives or ACE, I have recently joined Vistage as a member myself. This organisation, which works to an American concept, provides a monthly arena for up to sixteen members per group from non-competing organisations to meet for a training and development session. Each event has a speaker input session on a huge variety of subjects from NLP (Neuro Linguistic Programming) to accountancy and legal training, and a member problem-solving/resolving session facilitated by the group chair. This is not an inexpensive process and costs in excess of £12,000 per year. I am fortunate that my organisation foots the bill. But in terms of value it truly has to be experienced to be believed.

ACE provide a similar service, and both organisations are well worth looking into if you seek exposure to diverse training subjects along with first-class support from a unrelated peer group.

Many of the women I spoke to would happily choose from any of the following: a five-day business or strategy course – or longer – at a top business school; a PhD; an MBA from Harvard University; a better knowledge of finance. Meanwhile Natalie Douglas would prefer a better feel for people: 'I would like more emotional intelligence, to trust my intuition a hundred per cent and be able to read people.'

What do you think is the most important training?

TO DREAM THE IMPOSSIBLE DREAM

Some people wistfully wish for a qualification they simply can't have. Even in these days of equality there are still some things women cannot achieve, as Sue Catling, prospective parliamentary candidate for the Conservative Party, has discovered. Asked what qualification she would like, she frankly admits: 'An Eton education. Difficult for a woman, I know, but good contacts are the best possible qualification.'

The perfect qualification for Fiona Sheridan's job as a business risk partner in Risk Advisory Services at Ernst & Young would be mind-reading. In the absence of such a fantastic skill she would choose broader work experience and a greater exposure to business development techniques. Heather MacDonald also has a fantasy qualification on her wish list: 'If it were possible I would get a PhD in emotional intelligence, as that is what makes good leaders great. However, it is something you are born with rather than something that can be learned. To date there are no ways to qualify in the innate qualities like that which mean so much in management.' Sonita Alleyne's wish list is much more down-to-earth, but still tantalisingly beyond her grasp. 'I'd love the ability to say no to chocolate.'

Qualifications That Money Can't Buy

There's plenty of ambition out there to enhance life beyond the office. Perhaps because she has achieved all she wants in business terms Laurianne Enos yearns for a talent that's as far away from business management as you can get. To be a world-class pianist or an international footballer, she observes, is something money can't buy.

Over the Next Horizon

But there are plenty of women who are ready to tick the boxes of their ambition as soon as time allows. While Wendy Duckham, sales and marketing director of Construction Speciality UK Limited, has excelled in a traditionally all-male domain she has nonetheless identified one talent that would move her career still further forward: 'I would like to be able to speak a foreign language really well as this would open more doors for me.' Victoria Bannister, MD of Sportsshoes Unlimited, thinks the same way – and knows the language she would choose to be fluent in would be Chinese. Also seeking better understanding of fellow humans, Lesley Cowley would train to be a psychologist if she could.

Angela Hughes represents the approach of many successful

entrepreneurs when it comes to qualifications: 'I'd like a qualification in finance,' she admits, 'but that might make me a boring old git. I'm glad I don't have a qualification in sales though, because then I would have to follow the rules!' Ruth Spellman is sufficiently self-aware to spot a flaw in her management technique. 'I wish I was more evaluative,' she admits. 'Being headstrong, I do rush into things. But I always want to learn, to develop myself and get mentally stronger.'

Other Training Possibilities

Institute of Directors (IoD)

I have been a member of the IoD since 1989 and this world-renowned organisation provides training to international accredited standards. As well as organising conferences, it has wonderful facilities and networking opportunities. Considering the benefits, the fee is very modest and for those with no London offices their fabulous Pall Mall-based facilities are exceptional.

Chamber of Commerce

At a more local level, your Chamber of Commerce will provide a wide variety of training events. My experience is that although these tend to be less ambitious in scope, maybe lacking in cutting-edge inspiration, they nonetheless fulfil a need and provide a horses for courses programme. Costs tend to be very low considering the overall benefits.

MBA

Some of my interviewees, when asked what qualifications they wished they had, opted for the highly regarded MBA. Internationally recognised as the professional's professional qualification it is available on a full-time, part-time or even distance-learning basis from a large number of institutions. This is an academic qualification mostly delivered by academics affiliated in some way to a further education establishment and therefore much of the content can have a theoretical feel to it, which may put some people off. But it is very well regarded and can be a prerequisite for certain jobs. Depending on your own professional discipline you may get exemptions from certain modules. Costs vary and grants may be available, but by and large you will have little change from £10,000 per year.

Mentoring

Over the years I have been fortunate in having had access to various mentors – some of whom have been formal appointments through my employer, while others have been provided by benevolent and able peers and supporters.

Formal mentoring is a fairly structured process and can be provided on a variety of levels, and at any stage in your career. You can even take qualifications in mentoring, and if you like a structured process you may feel happier with this sort of support. I have enjoyed a less formal approach in as much as there has been no set agenda. I have met my mentors on a regular basis outside work, where I have had the opportunity to share, offload and detail specific and general matters concerning my career and even my personal life. These people have in varying ways helped me to deal with my self-doubts, skill deficiencies and career direction. Their insight, knowledge and encouragement (for me anyway) is better than anything I could have gleaned from a book or a classroom environment.

Clearly the skill is with the mentor, and fate has dealt me some exceptional people, but there are organisations which provide such personnel, and you should be able to assess their work in a relatively short period of time. Costs for this training and development are hugely variable from zero to astronomical for a professional, though you should expect to pay a minimum of £200 an hour for a mentor's services.

It took me some years to shake off the negative connotations attached to education. After that revelation, though, nothing could hold me back. It's all about looking outwards rather than inwards, upwards rather than sideways or below. Everything that's cultivated in the garden of the mind brings about a fruitful harvest at some time. Often education and self-development are difficult to avoid in a business environment. Accept that in business you are always learning – if you are not, you are not exposing yourself to the right process.

However, don't confuse a lack of education with inability. Sometimes courses and qualifications bring out inner qualities that were previously hidden, but many people have those strengths in abundance without needing a helping hand for them to flourish. It's vital to recognise those innate qualities that are the key to your success. As Helen Merfield noted: 'I wish I had realised a long time ago that who I am is sufficient.'

SELF-EDUCATION SURVIVAL GUIDE

■ Pursue knowledge for fun rather than financial reasons – don't be afraid of going 'off piste' with your training and development.

■ If the aim is career progression, choose your courses carefully. Not all courses will deliver your dreams. Investigate the possible outcomes beforehand so you are not disappointed.

■ Always ask your employer if they will sponsor and support your training needs, after all, if you don't ask you won't get!

■ Check out grants and subsidies attached to the course you have chosen.

■ Passing isn't everything, so don't get stressed about exam-based training. I have met some fantastic contacts just by participation.

■ Keep up to date with IT generally (ask your children/learn from your secretarial support/take a refresher course). Apparently, most of us use only 10 per cent of what Word and Excel are capable of.

■ Invest in the membership of groups and associations that will carry you on to quality courses.

■ Get a mentor.

■ My children, friends and relatives have passed me some wonderful tips on self-improvement and development.

CHAPTER 7

Getting Noticed

*When life hands you lemons, ask for tequila and salt
and call me over.*
Unknown

*I have noticed this about ambitious men or men in power
– they fear even the slightest and least likely threat to it.*
Mary Stewart, novelist

How do you stand out in the workplace?

Have an active role in business so people get to see you and to know you. Listening is just as important as talking to people. **Perween Warsi**

Smile and be positive. **Barbara Harvey**

Smile and look directly at people. **Nicola Kay**

You don't have to be loud or colourful to be noticed. Communicate lots and exude positivity. **Rolline Frewen**

Be tough but not confrontational. **Nicole Paradise**

Saying 'good morning' works. **Julie Kenny**

Create your own personal style, be open and welcoming, come up with solutions quickly and dispel the myth of being a dragon. In short, be a human being. **Deirdre Bounds**

Be comfortable in your own skin; this makes you charismatic. **Julia Moir**

Treat others as you would expect to be treated yourself. **Gail Carter**

Don't be a shrinking violet. **Deborah Adshead**

Volunteer! **Lesley Cowley**

Follow up and follow through. **Yvonne Lumley**

Don't undermine or patronise people for your own personal gain.
Hannah Evans

Get staff respect by knowing what you are talking about.
Barbara Scandrett

Look as though you mean business. **Fiona Vanstone**

If you have opposing views, express them without being negative, angry or personal. **Anon**

If you don't enter any awards, you won't win them. **Helen Merfield**

Stand tall, walk with confidence and ask questions. **Ann Worrall**

Listen to other people. **Lynda Hinxman**

Make the most of yourself. Laugh a lot. **Pooya Ahmadi**

Think on your feet, be imaginative and be yourself. **Clare Balding**

Say little but say it well. **Ruth Spellman**

Be yourself. It's normally enough to get you noticed. **Dianne Sharp**

Practice sound bites and speak well. That gives you credibility. **Sandra Brown**

On the whole, we humans are a modest bunch and women are often more self-deprecating than men. But there's nothing wrong with a bit of showboating, so long as it is executed with panache. Don't broadcast your successes in bland terms – that will irritate rather than ingratiate, but outlining achievements isn't a sin and isn't usually treated as such. Talking about past triumphs with a quiet voice and a steady gaze, without a hidden agenda, is perfectly acceptable in business. Usually you are the only publicist on your case.

This chapter deals with overcoming reluctance to self-promote by telling you how to make a splash, when and where, with tips from contributors and anecdotes on what self-publicity is good and what isn't so favourable.

Blow Your Own Trumpet

'You're such a show-off!' shouts the nine-year-old girl to her friend. 'I hate swots,' says the young boy to his mate. 'It would be better if we didn't mention our cruise round the Med,' says the wife to her husband.

Throughout our lives we have these real and imagined voices telling us not to boast of our achievements and triumphs. Our upbringing may lead us to believe that it's a sin to be successful and, if you are, you most certainly don't make a song and dance about it. It is not attractive to brag about what you have, particularly to those who may not be as fortunate as you for whatever reason, and it's even less acceptable if this is done in such a way as to make the other person feel inferior.

My own children have had untold privileges and I hope they are well aware of this. I have never missed an opportunity to remind them that there are many others who are not so fortunate. At worst I trust this has made them appreciative and at best a little humble when meeting those less well off than themselves. In my experience, however, men are less likely to display this self-deprecating type of behaviour. They are more likely to shout about their achievements than play them down.

It seems to me that the underplaying of achievements on a personal level is often replicated in the professional arena, creating in many cases a reserved aura. If, like me, you have siblings, you will have been repeatedly told to share: share games, toys, privileges – and even worse (with my sister) – clothes. In later life this behaviour results in sharing the limelight with colleagues. Not a problem and indeed expected for team efforts, but on those few occasions when it was truly a singular achievement, I still felt compelled to share. I did this because I felt it made me a better and a nicer person. But my more aggressive colleagues (male and female alike) haven't shared the limelight – they have stolen it! I have taken this behaviour on the chin and convinced myself I can rise above it, but in truth a niggle of self-pity has inevitably been hidden beneath the veneer of indifference.

Over the years I have come to the conclusion that professionally at least it is necessary to shout about your achievements. I will temper that by saying in the appropriate manner and time – but you do need to make it clear what you can do. Why? Because, frankly, false modesty can be as infuriating as the 'know it all – show it all'. Balance is clearly the key.

To achieve this balance, consider what is it you want to promote and why, i.e. what do you hope to gain from the activity?

Focus

The first question is, are you the brand or is your business the brand?

By and large in my business the brand has been me. My clients have bought Jo Haigh's skills and achievements. Naturally I am not able to deliver them without an effective organisation, but the latter supports the former, rather than the other way round. Once you have identified the focus, promotional activities in the correct direction are essential.

As any good marketeer will tell you, the next crucial element of a successful campaign is to have a clear idea of the desired outcomes. Is this simply awareness of you or your organisation as products, or is it rather about the engaging of the target audience? (This may be internal or external to the business.) It could be recognition of talent resulting in fast-tracking promotion, or it could be creating a buying signal, if it's a product you are promoting.

As this book is aimed at you, the individual, my tips and techniques are geared towards the professional self-promoting methods and models of operating and what works and what is less successful.

Awards

Competitions and awards have worked very well for me. Although some local authorities may have banned sports days to stop our offspring feeling the distress of coming second – or in my case, last –

it's impossible to erase competition from real life. When your child enters the big wide world of work, they will be in some sort of competitive position throughout their career, including industry, gender-generated or even nationwide competitions. Winning gives you a very nice feeling and a great sense of achievement. There are dozens of such awards and competitions nationally, locally and regionally, promoted by very prestigious organisations, including the IoD, CBI, Business Links and Chambers of Commerce.

My experience is that, sadly, few people apply, which provides you with an opportunity because potentially it reduces the odds. The bottom line is that if you don't take part you can't win or, in the parlance of my husband, 'You can't score if you don't make goal-scoring chances.'

I can't understand why more people don't apply for these things, is it lack of desire, lack of knowledge of the actual process, or is it fear of failure? Of course no one likes to lose and although I don't wholly subscribe to the philosophy that it is the taking part that matters, in my experience taking part has been very worthwhile indeed.

The following are some of the awards you might wish to apply for.

First Woman Award

The First Woman Awards recognise women who have broken new ground in business life – from entrepreneurs to corporate leaders to young pioneers; women who are trailblazers and pioneers in business – genuine 'glass ceiling breakers'. The First Women Awards are not just for general business achievement but for women whose achievement 'firsts' and individual actions have helped and are helping to remove barriers and open up opportunities for others to follow.

IoD Regional and National Director Awards

The IoD is comprised of a number of different regions who each organise their own award programmes. These awards are to celebrate the achievements of the best and most dynamic directors in the region, culminating in a lavish black-tie ceremony that attracts upwards of 400 attendees.

Chamber of Commerce – Regional Awards

The Chamber Awards were launched by the British Chambers of Commerce (BCC) in 2004 to recognise and celebrate business excellence through the successes and achievements of its Accredited Chambers of Commerce and their members.

As the only award scheme open exclusively to members of Accredited Chambers of Commerce, the Chamber Awards offer the chance for businesses across the UK to be recognised on a regional and national level.

Everywoman Award

The Everywoman Award celebrates inspirational businesswomen who have achieved significant success – particularly those who've had to overcome adversities such as financial constraints, social disadvantages or skills gaps. The awards play an invaluable role in both recognising success and inspiring other women to venture into the field of business.

Women 4 Business

Women4Business networking club is for women in business who would like to be more successful. It is a support network for Northamptonshire Women Business Owners. The networking club is a great opportunity to meet new contacts cost-effectively, promote your business and share your experiences and best practice with like-minded women.

The Women4Business awards recognise and celebrate the achievements of women who have started up their own business.

Women in Ethical Businesses Award

The Women in Ethical Business Awards (WEBA) aim to celebrate the women behind some of the most inspiring, ethical businesses in the UK. The WEBA winner will be an entrepreneur bringing ethical lifestyle choices into the mainstream – using business to make the world a better place. As well as wider recognition for their work, they will receive a specially tailored £2,500 business support package, providing practical help to move their business forward.

Prowess Awards

The Prowess Awards celebrate the female business owners who are giving a hand up to others, the dedicated supporters providing advice and mentoring, and the individuals and organisations who are shaping the women-friendly enterprise culture to the benefit of women and the UK economy. Together they are changing the face of enterprise.

Women and Technology Awards

The Women and Technology Awards recognise excellence and outstanding contributions to technology made by women. The eight categories recognise individual contributions to the corporate, public, SME and academia, as well as recognising the best female technology journalist and role model. Organisations also have the opportunity to take home an award on the night with a category recognising the technology company most committed to advancing female talent.

Women within the technology industry are achieving notable success and these awards have been designed to celebrate their achievements and increase their visibility. This extends to women performing non-technical roles within our industry, such as marketing or education, as well as those women outside the industry who are making effective use of technology to enhance their organisation's productivity and communications.

There are lots of regional and specialist industry awards as well.

The awards I have won have provided fantastic PR opportunities which help to endorse my credentials. Even those I haven't won have given me opportunities to promote myself. So the by-product is clearly one of accreditation, which in turn creates awareness and my own goal-scoring chances.

CV

If awards aren't your thing, don't be afraid to tell your story in the best possible and most positive manner. A good, well-constructed CV is a must if you are moving jobs. Get professional help with writing it and on layout. Develop a short profile of no more than five or six paragraphs, summarising yourself and your achievements. I am regularly asked for this. (Note to self, keep it up to date.)

Press

Your local and regional press can provide a marvellous forum for self-publicity. My experience has demonstrated that if you are willing to give your time freely and be proactive in creating a newsworthy editorial, they will bite your hand off.

I have done everything from writing a business problem page to monthly columns and quizzes. Build a relationship with the editors, give them ideas and kept it fresh.

Confidence

Put on your 'confidence cloak' whenever you are out and about professionally. I don't like the in-your-face man or woman who can't wait to tell you what they do, and how wonderful they are; we have all met these people at events over the years. There is clearly a critical difference between arrogance and self-publicity. A confident personality will make your peers generally feel more comfortable about your ability to deliver.

However, alongside this I would advise you to act in an appropriate manner when congratulated, a bit like when you are given a compliment. It can be very rude to pooh-pooh it, so accept such accolades politely and courteously.

Of course, there are other ways to be noticed apart from gathering awards, as some of my interviewees pointed out.

How do you promote yourself?

Natalie Douglas 'Dress the part and be a good actor. Use good body language. Don't be vulgar or loud.'

Rosemary Conley 'Shake hands and look the person you are meeting in the face. Remember people's names. Handwrite thank you notes. Most people are insecure but you can make them feel more secure and this will endear them to you.'

Tracy Viner 'Smile and make yourself approachable. Be real, be honest and be truthful.'

Denise Collins 'Be relationship-orientated and have plenty of one-to-ones in order to build relationships. A sense of humour and a sharp wit are fantastic for getting noticed. Be grounded and strategic and do the best job you can.'

Laurianne Enos 'Be everywhere, go to all events, get on forums, provide opinion. Create a buzz around yourself.'

Sarah Deaves 'Always embrace challenges and step up to the mark. Deliver advice in a fun manner and cultivate friendship. Women tend to take themselves too seriously in business.'

Joy Kingsley 'I am not quiet about what I have achieved. I don't boast, but I do inform. I work hard and have good ideas to put forward. I enter for loads of awards, not least as a public-relations exercise. More and more potential clients are asking what awards the company has won. This helps to develop both my personal and business brand.'

Rolline Frewen 'Gain respect by being true to yourself and honest with everyone else. You don't have to be loud or colourful to be noticed. Simply communicate lots and exude positivity.'

Sue Catling 'Really successful people are both scientist and artist. Their achievement is based not only on a deep understanding of their subject area but also on their ability to communicate confidently, to get their message over in a clear and interesting way, to sense the mood of their audience or client and to adapt their message accordingly.'

SELF-PROMOTION SURVIVAL GUIDE

- Look out for awards, gongs and other accolades that will raise your personal standing in your chosen field.

- Keep your CV up to date. Don't forget to include the self-improvement courses you've been on and the awards you've entered for or gained.

- When it comes to local press, think creatively and you could open up new corridors.

- Keep your contact database up to date with what you are up to.

- Always send personal thank you notes.

- Be confident.

- Help others if they lack confidence – they will never forget your assistance.

■ Become involved in a good cause be it a charity or a local initiative.

■ Showboat with style and no one will even be aware of what's happening.

CHAPTER 8

Lies, Damned Lies and Politics!

One of the penalties for refusing to participate in politics is that you end up being governed by your inferiors.
Plato

In war you can only be killed once, but in politics, many times.
Winston Churchill

How do you deal with gossip?

Betrayal hurts but don't lose sight of the real you or your dreams. Don't look down. **Nicky Pattinson**

Rise above it every time. Even when you know it's unfair and wrong, responding often validates gossip so it is always best to ignore it. **Nicola Kay**

Be whiter than white. **Barbara Scandrett**

I intervene, confirm it and deal with it. **Fiona Sheridan**

Put a shell around you to deflect the rubbish and only let the good come in. **Sandra Brown**

Behind every successful business there is usually a strong team that, tug-of-war style, pulls together in the same direction. That unifying spirit tends to bring out the best in everyone. But what if it doesn't? The truth is that even sound businesses can experience the ripples and undercurrents created by careless whispers.

We humans are far from perfect and one of our failings is the speed at which we resort to gossip and politicking, to the detriment of co-workers. Being successful does require a certain amount of political savvy. Women can be just as good as men but the 'bitch' gene planted in all of us along with the 'gossip' gene can dilute this positive skill. And even the best of us tells the occasional lie. Doctors, lawyers and vicars have been known to do it. Certainly, I must put my hand up when it comes to the odd fabrication.

This section scrutinises the signs of impending implosions, and recommends when to contribute – and when to watch.

Nothing But the Truth

Politics is not for everyone. In fact the political arena bores me rigid. The bickering and back-stabbing played out in the House of Commons when it is televised is enough to make me rapidly change channels. If politics includes deception and cover-ups then a desire to be part of that great game has never been on my radar.

Sadly there are low-grade political games taking place outside

Parliament in many offices across the nation. It's not fun, never reflects well and can be hurtful. Mostly it's done to elaborate or exaggerate the role of the protagonist.

Perception is so often in the eye of the beholder in the corporate world. What you seem to be is often worth more than what you actually are. Fluff, bumph and illusory enhancements have helped many an astute sales person achieve that elusive deal. Indeed sales training includes learning the skill of selling the 'sizzle' not the 'sausage', in other words the anticipation of what could be rather than what necessarily is.

My experience says that a large proportion of successful women have got excellent influencing and sales skills which by their very nature require the operator to be in tune with what the recipient finds desirable. Sucking up or brown-nosing is regarded by some as being politically savvy but undoubtedly it involves telling untruths. Beware this murky territory. I certainly wouldn't advocate being anything other than politely truthful even when pushed. If anything, being ultra-polite can give you a leading edge in an acrimonious situation. And anyway, is truth management really a positive attribute of the female manager or entrepreneur?

Some of the most successful people I have met have this behaviour pattern down to a fine art, particularly among the movers and shakers as they progress through the ranks. Often men seem more adept at this than women. I would suggest this is partly due to conditioning that provides for the survival of the fittest, and partly to their lack of desire to be a friend to everyone.

The trouble is this undoubted skill can give the activist a distinct advantage and, in the business race, they can leave you at the start line, hare and tortoise style.

My advice is to develop as quickly as possible an awareness of the political arena in which you are operating. It is true that lots of companies claim they operate an apolitical environment but I have rarely (if ever) been involved in a business where there was not some sort of political undertone.

In reality, if you are an employee, you may enter an already pre-aligned political circus. There's little you can do to change it; it presents its own difficulties because it may be a case of play or fail. If you are a business owner, it's left to you not only to create the politics but also to manage them in a corporate environment. As an owner-manager you will face protagonists who do not share your culture and that will happen more and more as your operation increases in size.

This game-playing is a skill you need to hone in order to be wary of too many falsehoods and fake praise – a savvy recipient will quickly pick up on any evident insincerity, especially if that recipient is another woman.

In building an empathetic potentially powerful relationship:

- Avoid clichéd statements of flattery.

- Don't be over-gushing.

- Be very careful indeed who you take into your confidence.

- Don't make promises just to please people if you are either not able or willing to carry them through.

- Know the 'terrorists' in your business and keep them close (closer than your 'friends').

- Treat all work-related events as just that – work.

■ If you mess up apologise to the right people straight away and in person (*not* by email).

■ Always have a plan B.

■ Develop the skin of a rhinoceros.

Such techniques will not make you totally foolproof or completely resilient but will at least put a reasonable fireguard round you and make you more attuned to what is effective.

The expression 'walls have ears' is one of those chestnuts to bear in mind if you play politics in an office environment. In my business life a few ill-directed words have caused me untold problems. One of the worst occasions of my career occurred when I was a young inexperienced manager in, of all places, the office lavatory. I had a conversation with a colleague about a member of my team, basically saying that person was not up to the job and would have to be coaxed out of the business. Imagine my horror when I later discovered the subject of the chatter was in the loo at the time and had heard every word!

Managing people is a skill that can be taught but some people are just naturally better at it than others.

You've Got Mail

The email revolution has created a culture of communication that has eliminated the need to make telephone calls or even speak directly to colleagues. I am as guilty as anyone of emailing colleagues who sit opposite me! It has also created an 'arse covering' culture. On average,

I receive a dozen emails a day which I have been copied in to or, even worse, blind copied in to often for no other reason than to show the main recipient that the sender wants to be seen to be informing the boss about their activity.

One client of mine has made Friday a 'no email' day and has removed the blind copy option from all emails. He recently told me that not only has this helped to dramatically improve the political environment, but he was also extremely enthusiastic about just how much quicker it was to pick up the phone or even, God forbid, walk round the desk and actually speak to someone face to face.

I must reluctantly agree with my technophobic husband who has told me for years that emails, although undeniably very useful, can cause trouble, where once none would have occurred. If being politically savvy means building close personal business relationships, a few ill-chosen words in an email are not only dangerous but also permanent. So –

- Avoid writing emails when you are mad or upset.

- Don't use capitals in an email as these infer you are shouting.

- Re-read before pressing the Send button. I have sent and received too many emails that appear abrupt to the point of rudeness, where none was meant.

Little Lies

My day job is corporate finance, which requires you to take a flexible approach to 'the truth, the whole truth and nothing but the truth'.

And, being brutally honest, all of us have told the odd white lie now and then – anything from a fake compliment about an ill-advised dress a friend has inexplicably chosen at great cost to her credit card or having the odd 'duvet day' while pretending to be sick.

Generally this manipulation of the absolute truth will do little or no harm, but my experience tells me that bending the truth is not at all the same as deliberately contrived lies. Not that I aspire to be some kind of moral superhero. Of course I have lied, I'd be lying if I said I hadn't, but more often than I would like these tales have come back to haunt me. However, be aware of the boundaries. Little lies have a habit of becoming big whoppers and can crucify a career.

Even the most highly regarded politicians have been caught short when their subterfuges have been discovered. For some it has brought their careers to an unnaturally early halt, although for others it has seemed to be no more than an agonising hurdle. The same scandals, sackings and resurrections happen in the business arena, and political double-speak is frequently at the heart of company life.

There have been occasions when a client has asked for details of experience in a particular sector and I have marginally exaggerated this, only to discover later that I have had limited exposure in this area and have had to learn on my feet. When I was younger I lied about my age at a job interview (saying I was older) because I didn't think they would take me on in the senior role for which I was applying. When I got the job they found out and it didn't go down too well. Now, of course, I'd rather chop off a few years than add them.

The trouble with lying is that you need a very good memory and, trust me, I do have one. But as all of us can carry only so much 'fake' information in our head, trip-ups occur, of course they do. On a recent foray into professional develop-ment, I went on a body-language course – absolutely fascinating and I highly recommend it. It's not an absolute science, but watch out for these telling signs of a liar:

- no eye contact

- hands over mouth

- rubbing ears or nose

- increase in temperature

- incoherent gabbling when confronted

- excessive overdenial when challenged

I have also found that men tend to have an inferior memory to women and soon contradict themselves.

Sometimes an appropriately placed lie is the right thing to do – yes, it is. Nobody wants to be told they look fat in that outfit, no matter how porky they appear. This is a cruel truth that's best kept under wraps. But excessive and unnecessary lying can and will get you into all sorts of trouble even when you have the best of intentions. You may recognise this scenario:

> A customer is desperate for goods. You are desperate to retain him and so over-promise on delivery. You fail to meet the agreed deadline. Result: lost customer.

Very simplistic I grant you, but you get the gist!

Gossip

The political culture in any business is hugely affected by the gossip chain. Now you could sit there and be holier than thou and say you do not engage in gossip, but forgive me if I challenge this assertion. You may, of course, try not to participate, or dilute its relevance by dressing it up as social communication in your mind. But whatever you do or call it, that ill-placed whispered statement is gossip.

Men do it, of course, but women, well, we are so much better at it! I am quite certain there is some deep-seated psychological reason for this but it's certainly got nothing to do with a bonding of the sisterhood. Often the gossip is not directed against a male colleague – an understandable target – but a female one. Quite why women seem to take pleasure in destroying their colleagues I can't say – but they do. Dare I say it's sometimes carried out with a delicious, malicious enjoyment.

Anon

People will always gossip. It's an informal method of communication that reveals a great deal. I confess to having been guilty of it myself. I take gossip with a pinch of salt and by nature I give people the benefit of the doubt. I'd like to believe I'm not alone in thinking like that. But when it's negative and getting out of order it's better to tackle it at source and put the record straight.

What I would say is that the more senior I have become, the less I engage in gossip and maybe this is a result of my increasing confidence. Belinda Earl, CEO of Jaegar, put it like this: 'I don't really do internal politics. There really isn't time.' Like her, I also find I'm just too busy to indulge in tittle-tattle on a regular basis. In fact what tends to happen now is that it's me they are gossiping about. Of course what I don't know can't hurt me personally, but that doesn't mean it can't affect my reputation internally and even externally.

This particular fact of gossip culture has actually encouraged me where appropriate to be an approved part of the gossip circle, not to actively participate but to keep 'in the know'. I try valiantly to refrain from gossipy corners but if I enter one it does allow me to set the record straight if not about myself then about other colleagues.

I've made mistakes in this area in the past. Now I *never* condemn anyone unless I am truly out of control. By and large I will be either impartial or actually highlight the positives of the person being attacked. This doesn't necessarily endear me to office gossips and may bring discussions to a swift end. The gossips may not like me much but that is hardly my main problem.

Women, myself included, take things very personally (by and large men don't seem to) and things said in passing can be hurtful and deeply upsetting. And it's far too slick and ambitious to say 'rise above it'. On a good day, you can. But on those days when you've had a row with the children, the plumber failed to turn up to mend the overflowing toilet and the train you usually catch to work was cancelled, this is difficult if not impossible.

Men move on, having a far greater skill than women in compartmentalising their business and personal life.

My husband sailed through his career, sublimely unaware of the scandalmongers and gossips. It could have been there weren't any, of course, but, being a realist, I just don't believe that. The fact is the gossip happened but it was just not on his radar.

167

Wounding Words

The theory is that you ignore gossip or that what you don't know can't hurt you. In practice it isn't always so. The effect of wounding words can be far-reaching, as some of my contributors revealed.

When Jeanette Sargent worked alongside her husband she was amazed and appalled at the level of gossip that perpetually surrounded the state of their marriage. 'There was even speculation we had split up when I wasn't wearing my engagement ring when in fact it was being cleaned . . . Nowadays I rarely comment, but, if I find it unacceptable, I will ask someone to stop. I am a believer in what you permit, you promote.'

Barbara Harvey thinks malicious gossip is like a slap in the face: 'Integrity in my job is very important to me. I would always confront gossips as I have a huge sense of injustice.' Dianne Sharp, MD of Mechetronics Limited, had barely been aware of office chatter until this year when rumours spread involving her and one of the managers. 'I was so angry,' she admits, 'I couldn't believe people would think I would behave in this way. I played them at their own game and circulated counter-rumours.' Gossip has been a challenge to Sue Catling and one she has found hard to handle. 'Successful women will always be the subject of speculation among those who are less talented while women continue to be vilified for characteristics which are considered admirable in men.'

Rising Above It

It may take time and not inconsiderable personal effort but you can rise above office gossip, as the women I interviewed proved. Christina

Vaughan used to be bothered by gossips but now she's resigned to the fact it will always happen. 'Focus your vision,' she advises, 'do not allow yourself to be distracted and rise above it. Don't lower yourself to respond either as it only gives the gossips credibility.' An anonymous contributor agrees: 'Ignore gossip. In extreme circumstances make a company announcement for clarification. The key is not to be distracted by negative activity like this or to take it personally.'

Stopping Gossip

There are some measures that can be instituted to prevent gossip from seeding. Dr Jane Guise went as far as removing all internal walls in the office to stop gossiping among staff. Outlawing loose talk may not stop it entirely but at least it broadcasts the standards that are expected.

Fiona Cruickshank explains that in her company, 'We have a code of conduct regarding behaviour and this type of thing goes against that code. We speak to people and ask them to stop. It usually works. And if not, well, they don't last long because our culture is not for them.' And if she is the subject of the gossip? 'I ignore it. It's a waste of my energy to do anything else.'

Hannah Evans says, 'I am fairly level-headed and not particularly sensitive to individuals who deal in these practices. Once you start getting involved it is a hard cycle to break – so best not to involve yourself. When faced with gossip my usual response is not to comment or react in any form. This tends to nip much of it in the bud as there is nothing for the gossipmongers to feed from.' While Wendy Duckham's method of silencing the gossips is simply to do a great job.

Listen Out, There's Information About

Some women, like me, like to keep one ear on office gossip to keep abreast of issues. Helen Merfield has a robust attitude towards gossip. 'My belief is that if I am important enough to be gossiped about, it's a good thing. As long as you know the real facts, there's no harm done. Most people can tell when others are gossiping. I pay no attention to this.' Deborah Adshead thinks there is another advantage as long as you are not malicious: 'A good gossip helps you find things out.' Rosemary Conley is likewise unfazed. 'What other people say about us is none of our business. Ignore it. If you are successful, people can be jealous. Be nice to the press because if you're not they can turn around and bite your bum.'

Anne Lockwood believes we are a nation of gossips – and we should take the chatter we pick up on the grapevine with a pinch of salt. Deirdre Bounds, CEO of i-to-i, keeps one ear on the company gossips. 'There may be some truth in what they are saying. Sometimes I must accept that there is no smoke without fire.'

OFFICE POLITICS SURVIVAL GUIDE

- Be politically savvy. That doesn't mean nasty and backstabbing, rather maintaining an awareness of what's going on around you.

- Don't brown-nose. The advantages of playing up to the boss are limited, while the potential perils are many.

- Be brave, be bold but don't be bolshie. Office strops are political hot potatoes.

- Avoid gripes by email. As your words whizz around the universe they gather more and more momentum. It's better to seek face-time for whining.

- When it comes to gossip, listen but don't take part. The ripples following spur-of-the-moment character assassinations sometimes turn into tidal waves.

- If you are the subject of gossip, deal with it promptly and with good grace.

- Don't take sides against colleagues.

My conclusion would be – keep in touch with the gossip channel, manage and be aware of the participators, rectify blatant lies and support those who need it. A view expressed by some of the women I interviewed was 'least said soonest mended' and no doubt this view has merit. In many ways gossip can be compared to the daily tabloid scandal, with yesterday's news being just that, but I do think there is a difference between this and the ostrich syndrome. Burying your head in the sand is not the answer. As Pooya Ahmadi says, 'Integrity is the most important thing.'

One great technique that a very successful entrepreneur I know uses when he (yes – sorry it's a bloke) joins a new business is to give everyone – and I mean everyone – a pack of yellow, green and red Post-it notes. He then asks them to write on the red anything they want him to stop doing, on the yellow things they want him to do and on the green, those things they want him to do more of. Only when he achieves success in these areas in their minds are the Post-it notes removed – by the people who put them there. All these are put up anonymously and are all over the place – even in reception! Without exception, people are drawn to him by his disarming honesty. A brave man, but also a very successful one.

CHAPTER 9

In passing, also, I would like to say that the first time Adam had a chance, he laid the blame on a woman.
Nancy Astor, politician

Too much of a good thing can be wonderful.
Mae West, actress

What is your advice for managing women?

Accept you need to be flexible in working hours and commitments.
Alison Boxall

It doesn't matter whether you are managing male or female staff. The important thing is the style you use, and that style has to be flexible.
Perween Warsi

Nurture the relationship and be professional. **Denise Collins**

Make women feel part of the team. **Justine Dignam**

Be fair and have empathy. **Nicola Kay**

Deal with people as individuals. **Julia Moir**

Treat everyone on the basis of what they contribute to the business rather than gender, race, educational background or sexuality.
Christina Vaughan

Never divulge confidences. Do what you say you are going to do but remain slightly detached. **Anne Lockwood**

Set firm business and behavioural objectives to stop teams getting toxic. **Yvonne Lumley**

Be yourself and don't feel as if you're competing. **Jeanette Sargent**

Use sensitivity if you have to be critical as women can take things very personally. **Clare Balding**

Be a good listener, develop rapport and make women feel included.
Gail Carter

Once, women tended to be poor managers of other women. The successful few looked down from their lofty precipices and were concerned about guarding empires, shoring up shaky positions and maintaining a macho image. This translated into fairly brutal management techniques and successful women became another brick in the wall. Thus there was a time when women preferred to be managed by men.

This is changing, though, and fast. As more women climb towards the glass ceiling the atmosphere up there is becoming more convivial. The desire, in the name of survival, to ram a stiletto into the face of those women approaching in our wake is all but gone. If we are to help our female colleagues survive and climb the ladder, recognising this negativity, managing it and then eliminating it is essential.

This section deals with coping and management techniques women can learn and introduce into their management style.

Sisterly Support

I'm going to make a confession now about an incident that I have filed away in the dusty lockers of my mind for years. Even the thought of it makes me break out into an uncomfortably guilty sweat. But this book is nothing if not honest, so here goes.

It all happened a long time ago. One of my first directorships in a rapidly growing company meant I needed to recruit a number two, a brand new role that would provide a challenge and plenty of opportunities for the incumbent. At the time I was not only the sole female director, but also the only female on the whole senior management team. We clearly lacked balance and, although positive discrimination had not yet been coined as a phrase in management speak, this was obviously a golden opportunity to improve the gender ratio of the company.

I recall I interviewed a number of very eligible candidates, male and female, but one woman stood out head and shoulders above the rest. It should have been a no-brainer. The common sense thing to do was to hire her, the best person for the job, quickly before she was snapped up elsewhere. The trouble was, she was bloody gorgeous! A natural blonde, she had curves in all the right places. If that wasn't bad enough she was smiley, empathetic and super-intelligent. Guess what? I turned her down. The reason was straightforward enough and, I suspect, not uncommon. I felt threatened by her potential presence in the company.

It's not an episode I'm proud of and I know I would never act in such a juvenile manner again. It troubles me greatly that if I sank to such low standards, how many other able and talented women were stone-walled in business in that unenlightened era?

Now everything has changed, I'm delighted to report. Compromises on candidates are rarely made today. As the women I've interviewed for this book often chorused, always recruit the best you can afford and preferably people more talented than yourself. As Joy Kingsley, MD of Pannone LLP says, get stars and retain them. While I haven't always followed that advice in the past, I do now and ensure I pull in the best applicant who's out there.

As my confidence has grown over the years, I am comfortable with this requirement. At last the qualities traditionally brought to top-level management by women are being celebrated rather than sidelined. In fact, an entirely different way of operating is now in vogue, thanks to women executives who are making changes from the top down in some of the world's biggest companies.

One oft-quoted example is Anne Sweeney, who has been elevated to the very upper echelons of Disney-ABC Television, which one might imagine to be something of a brutal arena best suited for gladiatorial combat. If it was once, it certainly isn't any more. Sweeney has won a reputation as a listener who's always prepared to share the spotlight. In order that employees satisfy her mantra of 'create what's next', she is meticulous about giving everyone enough space to be imaginative and original. Indeed, she hosts coffee mornings to hear feedback from workers about how they are functioning within company constraints. Her buzzwords are kindness and curiosity. Even when she's angry she maintains her dignity. 'I don't go blazing into a room, knocking everyone down round me, but just sit down and hold my position.'

In an interview with the *Observer* on 10 June 2007 she explained how nurturing her autistic son had been a model for her approach to employees.

I don't expect them to come in with all of the answers: there's a lot of learning that needs to go on for people to be successful, so I don't create impossible bars for people to jump over. I make sure the task at hand or the idea to think about is laid out very clearly. And I make sure I've got people on board, and I give them enough freedom to experiment, but always make sure that I'm guiding them.

In the 1980s the number of female high-fliers was few and most felt they had to act like men to stay ahead of the game, witness Margaret Thatcher. These days politicians have another face. Jacqui Smith, the Home Secretary whose appointment in the summer of 2007 coincided with two domestic terrorist attacks, is known for her calm, charming and even-handed approach to the job. The first ever woman Home Secretary in Britain, she is bringing equanimity and ease to the demanding role, while still being politically tough.

It's been the same story in the commercial world. I'm sure all readers can identify a woman in industry who made it to the top a few years ago and became more macho than the men surrounding her. Thankfully, she's yesterday's woman. As a survey in *Management Today*, published on 1 July 2007, pointed out: 'Whereas once it was thought queen bees stung those women around them, it would now seem that the nectar is shared out between the women workers.'

Deborah Adshead is among many who believe women who are trying to be men have no place in management: 'Try to be nurturing and find out about your employees' personal triggers. Allow women to fulfil their own dreams. Be flexible and open to women's needs. Don't be aggressive, rather encourage creativeness.'

Julie Kenny CBE, MD of Pyronix Ltd

So often in life you need a leg-up. Two men in my life have given me chances. I grabbed them but would I have created them? Now I am always looking to fill the capacity behind me with a woman. Women bring a different dynamic to a meeting and the more of those you have, the more the organisation benefits . . . Don't be sad because people want to leave and grow. They can still return and bring so much back with them.

It's never wise to generalise, but once men at the top used to play hard ball to illustrate to superiors above and ambitious employees below that they were a force to be reckoned with. Now different qualities are lauded as the most effective way to run businesses.

We Are Family

As women gain respect in the wake of excellent work in top jobs, so the attitude towards family commitments is changing. Once a culture of work first meant women and men alike were reduced to neglecting or even denying their families. Now that's changing. Mothers with sick children no longer need to skulk out of the office. Fathers of newborn babes can spend time at the crib with pride, secure in the knowledge that their job is not in jeopardy. Many employers reap benefits from this new family-first approach. Says Victoria Bannister, 'Be flexible and understand family and child-centred issues. You will get paid back ten times over.'

How to Lose Friends . . .

I've never worked for a woman and sometimes I wonder what differences there would be with a woman boss. Socially, I have a small group of selected, special friends who are supportive, fun and who make it their business to keep me grounded. All of them are women. I'm not saying I would die for them or vice versa, but on balance I believe I would go pretty much the whole nine yards and I feel certain this is reciprocated. Together we have lived through each other's traumas, ups and downs, highs and lows. We have drunk gallons of wine and cried buckets of tears, as well as bitched, gossiped and laughed our way through many years. As it happens, most of my special friends have careers similar to my own, not the same professional discipline but basically we all hold comparable roles in industry. This means we can relate to the pressures felt by the others.

Would I want to work for them or even with them? Almost certainly,

I think we would all say a resounding NO. For one thing, mixing close friendship with business is almost always catastrophic. Of my five closest girlfriends three of us, including me, made this mistake (not with each other I hasten to add) and in each case it cost us a life-long friendship – a hard lesson.

Female of the Species

Then there's the thorny issue of feminine wiles. Have I ever resorted to fluttering eyelashes or a pout to seal a business deal? Well, probably, if I felt it would further my cause, but there's no doubt that this rather unsound approach would not work among women.

'It helps not to look better, younger, thinner or richer than female clients. If it looks as if you have the perfect life they are going to hate you,' says Kate Ancketill. But on a more serious note, she believes that women's natural warmth works wonders in the businesses environment. And at last the women's network is sufficiently widespread to be exploited. And she's found another advantage to employing predominantly female staff: 'I have never come across a man who would wash up – all my staff would.'

Working for or alongside women demands altogether different tactics. With my female clients I have found it essential to be empathetic, reassuring and to give congratulatory praise and support to build relationships. Most of these women have also been far more demanding than their male counterparts and like to point out errors and faults. But on the other hand they have been ultimately more forgiving of mistakes, particularly if I have acknowledged the fault and speedily rectified it. The sisterly camaraderie you may imagine exists in such relationships has in my case not been present.

Natalie Douglas faced a dilemma when she joined IDIS as a market-ing manager. 'Lots of people stood in my way when I joined IDIS. They saw me as threatening and didn't like my drive and ambition – and all of them were women. I found them very bitchy and they wouldn't make tough decisions. I overcame it by proving myself and ultimately buying the business.'

With female peers outside my department I have been fortunate indeed in being able to form good supportive business friendships and bonding against whatever adversity we are dealing with at the time.

Vive la Difference

The fence that separates men and women at work is being eroded but there are still differences between the sexes that stand out when it comes to management.

Joy Kingsley is used to dealing with women. Not only is there a raft of secretarial staff at her company but half the fee-earners, half the partners and one-third of the equity partners are women. 'I recognise that women have different skills. Women can multi-task, for example, while men do one project at a time. Women are emotional, men less so. Women are generally more upset by criticism.' The way forward, she believes, is by getting to know everyone's motivations and framing management around it.

'Women have less hang-ups than men, and the way forward is to forgive the ones they do have. Men shout, are angry, combative and competitive. Women have "baby" needs reflected as tears, stomp outs or sulks. You need to appreciate this and give them a hug. But if they do it too much, they need to grow up,' says Barbara Harvey. While Tracy Viner thinks that 'Women need you to be honest. They read faces better. If you can't be honest, don't bullshit.' Sarah Deaves points out that women are people and everyone is different. Still, she flags up that women tend to have more empathy than men. Indeed, she says: 'Women are very generous and self-deprecating.' Dr Jane Guise admits that she finds men easier to manage because they ask fewer questions.

Anita Brough, sales and marketing director of Russell Richardson & Sons Limited, thinks there needs to be two different approaches: 'You can be straightforward and blunt with a man, but you need to be aware of emotions and watch how you speak to a woman.' Christine Booth acknowledges a difference between managing men and women. 'I inherited a female team. With men you can be direct and blunt but with women you need to think carefully about how you feed back.'

How do you manage women?

Ann Worrall 'Women need to off-load and need more one-to-one time so you can listen and then help them build their performance and create an arena that's safe and confidential for them to do this. Give praise and notice people and take action.'

Sue Catling 'Be supportive. Recognise that they may be juggling several balls like you. Protect their confidences but never, ever share your own.'

Pooya Ahmadi 'Understand that women are more sensitive and think more laterally. Women are less secure.'

Nicky Pattinson 'Business people can be very lonely. I'm lonely. Sub-consciously we are all looking for a family to belong to. Make people feel an emotional anchor to your company.'

Wendy Duckham 'I speak to every one [of my employees] on a level, recognise emotional issues and talk about their emotions.'

Fay Sharpe 'Use empathy, an open approach, trust, respect, set clear goals together and make sure you praise good work publicly.'

Diana Green 'Be professional and supportive. I encourage women into senior roles. I create an environment that supports women. I think mentoring is vital for everyone and women especially need more encouragement.'

Fiona Sheridan 'I like to think I can make a difference to women in the workplace, but it's a hell of a responsibility.'

Office Equality

Soon men and women will genuinely claim equal status as gender bias is eroded to nothing. For some, that's already happened. Heather MacDonald points out, 'Everyone has masculine and feminine characteristics, traits and behaviours and it is those that you have to learn to successfully manage in both men and women.'

One woman boss told me that most people regardless of gender respond to praise and having their opinions considered: 'Treat women – and men – with respect and encourage them to aspire to all they can be.'

With female junior colleagues I tend to take a nurturing or mentoring position, possibly because I don't feel threatened, but I would like to think I am being altruistic, though maybe it's more maternal. What is strange is that I do not tend to have the same attitude towards my male colleagues. One wonderful interviewee told me, 'The best thing a successful woman can do is to help another woman.' Whenever I have, the results have been paid back many times over. Not in gratitude, although of course that is nice, but in seeing just how far that woman can go. My PA has recently become a qualified accountant. She has done this all by herself, but I like to think it was through my encouragement that she embarked on the programme and she has certainly had my support throughout. I am genuinely thrilled by her achievements.

As any good NLP instructor will tell you, in order to improve your success, you need to understand and mirror your client, colleague or peer in behaviour. Sometimes we do this naturally and sometimes we need to work at it. It has taken me years to deal with the demons that threatened my management ability and, frankly, I am not sure they have all been annihilated, but at least I am more aware of these failings.

♀

SURVIVAL GUIDE FOR
MANAGING WOMEN

■ Give women a helping hand. There's no finer legacy to leave in business.

■ Accept that there are differences between men and women at work but do not be ruled by that premise.

■ Treat all colleagues and employees equally.

■ Be professional, effective and confident at work – and be a model for female junior executives.

■ Remember flexibility in the working day is hugely valued by most women.

■ A thank you or a word of praise to another woman for a job well done is worth more than mere monetary awards.

■ Hormonal patterns are often mirrored in female-dominated offices; if you feel moody/homicidal/suicidal then probably most of the office is feeling the same!

CHAPTER 10

Do a Frank Sinatra

Psychologists think that those who are early are anxious, those who are late are aggressive and those who are always on time are compulsive.
Psychologies *magazine*

Thirty-five is when you finally get your head together and your body starts falling apart.
Caryn Leschen, artist

What are your top tips for creating a successful enterprise? (Part 2)

Having ambition and passion, a drive for success and a shared mission are all important. **Heather MacDonald**

Acknowledge your support network and say thank you. **Tracy Viner**

Always go with your gut instinct and get a great human resources director. **Helen Merfield**

Think small in the beginning and grow. **Ruth Spellman**

Have the edge on competitors. Get there before anyone else. And just do the best you can, whether you are the cleaner or the CEO. **Angela Hughes**

You can't always be right. Live and learn. Create a culture people aspire to work in and live those values from the top down. **Fay Sharpe**

You need a business that suits you, especially when the going gets tough. **Barbara Scandrett**

Keep everyone happy and motivated. **Fiona Vanstone**

Do things differently and always keep your commitment. **Pinky Lilani**

Be confident and energetic. **Fiona Cruickshank**

If in doubt, sleep on it. Don't gamble your business. **Victoria Bannister**

Have a team around you who enjoys themselves. **Dr Jane Guise**

Do something you enjoy as you will be spending a lot of time doing it. **Nicole Paradise**

Do your billing on time and read a couple of good body-language books. I still make mistakes . . . But the greatest mistake is not to move on. Don't allow it to consume you. **Nicky Pattinson**

My dad told me I could be anything I wanted to be. I sneaked in the back door – isn't it great? **Dianne Sharp**

Nobody said it was going to be easy. But sometimes finding your way to the top of a corporate or large company is all but impossible, not because of a lack of talent but because the established path is littered with obstacles that are difficult to overcome. Some people stay and take a sledgehammer to those obstacles. Others opt for a new road, the one heading towards self-employment because, if all else fails, the only way to succeed may be to do it your own way, alone. No longer will you be shackled by the chains that bind women in large corporations, but neither will there be the safety net that employment brings woven with holiday and sick pay and a guaranteed salary. Maybe the sacrifices will be worthwhile. This section contains anecdotes from those professional women who have fashioned their own future by going it alone.

Go Your Own Way

I started my first business under the foolish misapprehension that I would have more time for my family . . . boy, what a mistake that was. Time was one thing that vanished at an alarming rate. When you work for yourself it's a 24/7 schedule, particularly in the early days. But still, I had the ability to control the use of my own time, which was a fantastic positive. No longer did I need permission to attend the nativity play, sports day or even have a sneaky afternoon off. Of course I made up the time for these jaunts and the rest, but at least I could do it.

Another reason for starting my own business was that I was absolutely fed up with making everyone else I worked for seriously wealthy, while I just drew a salary. Somebody once observed: 'You will never get rich working for someone else.' In the main, I believe that to be the case. Real wealth (if that is an important motivator for you) can only be gained by creating an entity with an inherent value. Of course, such processes are fraught with problems and there is absolutely no guarantee whatsoever of success. With one in three businesses failing in their first year, running your own business is not something to enter into without serious consideration.

When I started in business on my own I gave up a very good salary, a company car and all the usual executive benefits. All the time I was employed I received a pay cheque every month and my expenses were paid in full. Even when the firm I worked for had bad times, salaries were always a priority. Not so when it's your own business. Of course I always paid everyone else, but there were many months – too many months – when I wasn't paid anything at all. Instead, I put all the available money back into the business to keep it afloat.

I was lucky: I had a husband with a good job who supported me and it was, I admit, something of a crutch. Although he never bailed me out, I was at least secure in the knowledge that the mortgage would always be paid and there would be food on the table. This is not a privilege all female entrepreneurs will have.

In my case, my business flourished and provided me with a great return, both financially and emotionally. But I had my fair share of disasters along the way and lots of sleepless nights. Some of my catastrophes have been the excruciating sort, which make you bury your head under the nearest pillow. There was the time I was chairing an IoD conference when, between speakers, I decided to get a tissue out of my bag. I promptly dropped the bag on the floor and an entire box of tampons scattered under the feet of the nearest members of the audience. Or the occasion I went to the loo with my microphone still switched on during a training event. Or when I insisted to the car-park attendant that my car had been stolen because it was not on level 5 where I had left it. Too late I discovered it was parked on level 4 and the figure 5 I thought referred to the level was actually the speed limit. Or when I spoke to William Hague at a Chamber of Commerce function believing him to be an old friend of mine. Confident of bonds built up over the years I said, 'It's so rude of me but I just can't remember your name.'

For all the comical and embarrassing moments during my career, I have still been successful and, indeed, often these episodes have grounded me. One of the biggest drivers for me has always been my desire to show those who thought I couldn't be successful that I could and would be despite all manner of mishaps. I badly wanted to show a number of misogynists I had met along the way that I could succeed in the face of their dark predictions of failure. More than a handful of men during my early career had told me I couldn't make it on my own, that I hadn't the guts or the staying power. It wasn't always said outright, although I do recall a male colleague informing me that I would never be taken seriously in corporate finance, a career even now not overpopulated by women but in those days I was something of a lone ranger. 'Your clients – if you get any – will almost all be men,' he observed. 'Why on earth would they take advice from a woman?' Of course he was partially right – some didn't, but thankfully lots more did.

Some of the women I interviewed started their own business out of desperation as a result of bullying or being blocked for promotion, some because of a need to survive financially or otherwise. Most had made huge sacrifices in a bid to succeed that went beyond financial hardship. I want to share with you the stories of two inspiring women.

CASE STUDY

Julia Gash, founder and director of Gash UK Ltd

In the mid-1990s, Julia Gash was a fashion designer with buoyant markets in the Far East and one of Sheffield's leading business-women. She won export awards, showed Princess Anne round her factory and had tea at Buckingham Palace. Then in 1997, the Asian economy collapsed, taking 93 per cent of her business with it. She lost her home, her cars and her eleven-year relationship. Turning her back on the rag trade she decided her best oppor-tunities lay with sex. Not sordid or saucy sex, but the sort most women indulge in – or want to – without being made to feel ridiculous. In 2000, she launched Gash, a website and shop specialising in erotica. It's more than just a sex site now. Regular Gash events include erotic writing evenings, striptease classes and courses in self-defence. In May 2004 *Cosmopolitan* gave Julia a 'sex salute' in recognition of 'her services to womankind'. The business has grown by 40 per cent year on year.

'There's a real surge of women entering the sex industry and of sisters doing it for themselves,' Julia told the *Observer* on 20 June 2003. 'There's been such a turnaround in attitudes, and programmes like *Sex Tips for Girls* and *Sex and the City* have been a driving force. Samantha is such an icon ... It's de rigueur to have a vibrator – a sign of autonomy, a zeitgeist thing. The result is a big bandwagon of women selling sex while waving the female-friendly banner.'

Julia's new business started with the collapse of her relation-ship and a trip out to buy a vibrator. 'I'd had quite a sheltered sex life and knew there was something missing,' she says. 'I went into a licensed sex shop with blacked-out windows, fluorescent lighting and wall-to-wall porn and came out with a brown paper bag, feeling I'd committed a crime. It took two weeks to get it out of its packet, and when I finally found out how good it was, I kept thinking how different the shopping experience could have been. I realised there must be a whole nation of women like me out there.'

She is also known for charitable work. 'I've kick-started many different initiatives, such as the Ab Fab Charity Fashion Show, the Devonshire Quarter Traders Association, the Gash Girls Parties and more. They've all brought me in contact with lots of different people and have really raised my profile. It takes time and energy, but once you've got the ball rolling it goes along by itself. I now find I'm included in many guest lists because of the innovative community-based work that I did through my business.'

It's the story of a surprising business success from a woman whose mission was to build an empire not only rooted in sales but also in women's empowerment.

CASE STUDY
Sandra Brown OBE, founder of the Moira Anderson Foundation

Sandra Brown had startlingly different reasons for instigating her venture. She began a charity foundation after suspecting her father had been involved in the abduction and murder of a child.

When she was young Sandra was told her father, Alexander Gartside, was in a hospital where 'children couldn't visit'. In fact he was serving a sentence for the rape of a young babysitter. While he was on bail prior to his conviction for this crime Moira Anderson disappeared, in 1957.

Late one February afternoon eleven-year-old Moira set off on an errand, wearing a pixie hat and navy-blue gabardine raincoat, intending to buy her mother a birthday surprise. She was last seen in a bitter blizzard getting on a bus driven by Sandra's father. Her body has never been found. Moira's parents died broken-hearted, never knowing what had happened to their daughter. At the time Alexander Gartside's own father was convinced his son had been involved in the killing and ripped up the floorboards of the family home looking for the body.

A chance remark by her father at a family funeral, following a long estrangement, convinced Sandra he was the killer of Moira Anderson. Later still, a deathbed confession made by another paedophile put the blame on Gartside, and two others pinpointed the child's burial site and talked about an active paedophile ring involving men in the upper echelons of Scottish society. Gartside died in 2006 without making a public confession, and surviving family members insist he is innocent. Police still consider Moira's disappearance a 'missing persons' case.

Sandra has written a book and a play about her experiences, revealing some of the trauma she felt on discovering her father was capable of a shocking crime. 'Some people think I am obsessed,' she told the *Scotsman* on 25 June 2006. 'I'm not, but I am a driven person. I want the truth. And I will keep up the pressure. I'm not giving up.'

To ensure Moira's name would not be forgotten Sandra started a foundation in 2000 based in Airdrie to help tackle child abuse. She was awarded the OBE for her work in 2006. She also runs a training consultancy called Potential Plus. Few business pioneers have such pressing and emotive reasons as this to start an enterprise. However, the personal imperative can be overriding as both Julia and Sandra demonstrate.

Building Your Business

Having your own business doesn't necessarily mean creating a huge and profitable empire, because, without doubt, self-employment is not all about money.

Several of the female entrepreneurs I met were being paid far less than the market rate by their own companies, but felt the flexibility of being their own boss and a real sense of personal achievement more than compensated for a reduction in remuneration. Naturally you will need to find your own balance – after all flexibility is one thing, but most of us need a certain level of funds to survive.

If you do go down the self-employment route, don't expect any favours because you are a woman. If my experience is anything to go by, the opposite will be the case. Financiers were sceptical, as were clients, and I constantly had to overdeliver. One thing I learned quickly was to underpromise, in other words I was super-cautious with what I claimed I could achieve and then was able to impress when I improved on this. Of course balance is the key – be too cautious and you won't secure the client, funds or whatever, be too optimistic and potentially you fail before you start.

After many years of working with countless companies, I have gained a huge insight into what makes a business more or less successful. When I started my own company, I had no such experience. Many basic techniques can easily be learned and I have tried to share whatever pearls of wisdom I have garnered in my previous books: *The Business Rules* and *Buying and Selling a Business: An Entrepreneur's Guide*. But in truth, I think most of us learn what works and what doesn't as we go along.

Some people have asked me why they haven't been told about a particular business issue or problem in the past. The reason is usually that they haven't asked. The problem is, however, that you may not know what you don't know and therefore don't ask the right questions! Also, of course, there is the potential scenario that if you did know you might not have taken that initial leap in the first place!

Support

Building a business is one thing, building a sustainable, successful one is quite another. My interviewees provided me with lots of tips, but the overriding theme was one of focus and determination. 'Never give up' was a phrase I heard numerous times regarding the pursuit of success.

I have previously alluded to the great support network you need to be successful and I am fortunate in my own group of friends and colleagues. But at the end of the day, when you close your eyes, you are alone with your thoughts and you do need great self-reliance, which is not a trait many people and particularly many women have.

Quite a few of the women I spoke to not only ran their own companies, but had no domestic support at all. Many of them had a number of dependent children or elderly parents and sometimes even dependent siblings. These women enjoyed huge personal strength and stamina, the latter being something anyone who has their own business must have by the bucket load. They live by the saying: sleeping is for wimps.

Seriously though, you simply will not be allowed too much downtime in the early days of your venture, and you need to prepare yourself physically and mentally for this change of pace.

One of Frank Sinatra's most famous songs was 'I Did It My Way' and adopting this mantra will give you a huge sense of achievement. But, take it from somebody who did it her way that, although the path is now well and truly carved out for the professional woman, it is by no means well trodden and you need to walk it with extreme care and an open mind. But it is possible to clear your own road somewhat, if you take on board some of the following advice.

GOING YOUR OWN WAY SURVIVAL GUIDE

■ A start-up business is much more likely to fail than buying an established company (provided you buy at the right price of course!).

■ Becoming a franchisee is a hugely popular option and has a massive success rate attached to it.

- Don't go into any sort of partnership or co-ownership without the required documents in place, such as partnership or shareholder agreements. Think of these as prenups!

- Don't underfund or overgear your business too soon unless you are pretty certain you can trade through it. Businesses fail through lack of cash, not lack of profit. Remember: sales are vanity, profit is sanity, cash is absolutely bloody essential!

- Surround yourself with the best advisers, staff and management you can afford.

- Have clearly defined goals and objectives that you monitor and check.

- Get a non-executive director as soon as possible.

- Have a clear sales proposition:
  – cheap and cheerful or
  – quality and value for money
  but never send out mixed messages.

- Tame your funders as soon as possible, but always keep them in the picture – good or bad.

- Celebrate success and be pragmatic about mistakes – but learn from them.

- ■ Create a brand and capital value if you want to create long-term worth or live well off the business. Note that it's either or – it's not possible to have both.

- ■ Have good-quality financial and management information available, including regular freeze-frames, i.e. flash figures on critical areas and more robust monthly management accounts.

- ■ Get into the discipline of having regular board meetings.

- ■ Surround yourself with 'what and why' men and women, not 'yes' ones.

- ■ Take risks (preferably calculated ones) but depend on your 'riskdar'.

- ■ And, finally, don't forget that the only people who don't fail are those who don't try.

Perween Warsi, founder and chief executive of S&A Foods

First and foremost it is about having a vision. However, putting the vision into practice is the key to making it a success. It's often important to share that vision with other people to ensure it works. If you don't share your vision it may just remain a dream. My vision was to have as many people as possible in the UK eating high-quality Indian cuisine.

Inspiring people with your vision and your values is arguably the greatest motivator there is. Second is innovation. I can't think of a single business which doesn't need to constantly be thinking of the next big idea or how they can develop their product further. Without innovation a business will stagnate. However, with a creative and progressive team working with you, the world is your oyster! Third, I would say determination. Everyone needs determination and a drive to succeed. Without this your business won't move forward. A determined team working towards a common goal is a recipe for success. Finally, think about people. People are the biggest asset in my company. Without them S&A Foods would not be where it is today.

People

If people make a business then good people make a successful business, one you will be proud to roll out beneath you. The women I spoke to, all successful and experienced, were as one on this subject. Sarah Deaves thinks that 'People *are* the business. Unlock their ideas and talents across the company. They frequently know the answers, but need to be encouraged to voice them. If you can tap into this it will turbo-charge your own performance.' Sue Catling believes that you need to be 'sufficiently confident in your own strengths to surround yourself with excellent people who plug your weaknesses'. Ann Worrall, MD of Stokvis Tapes, also pays tribute to people power and looks for those who have complementary skills to her own. 'Communicate and make them feel part of the business. I'm not charismatic but I am inclusive.'

For Lesley Cowley, the key to success is simple: 'Look after the people and the cash.' The strength of Wendy Duckham's enterprise has also been in the people around her. 'Employ people you like,' she advises. 'Ask "why not?" rather than "why?".' An anonymous contributor followed the same vein: 'Understand that people make the difference. Go the extra mile for individuals and they will repay you ten times over.'

Daring to Dream

Ambition also plays its part. Without a vision for the future your business will trundle along on a road to nowhere.

With one eye on her own success Christina Vaughan is in no doubt that it's the people on her payroll who have helped her along the way. Her advice to others is 'employ great people and give them room to succeed'. However, she has kept her sights on success throughout.

I have grown a business from one person to almost ninety in less than seven years. We have offices in four countries with distribution through more than 200 outlets in eighty countries. Our images today generate gross sales of more than 40 million dollars. It has been hard work but also an absolute pleasure and privilege. Many people are surprised when they learn I am a woman, still relatively young and from an ethnic-minority background. I grew up in a working-class household in Sheffield. However, I believe the success of the business has come from daring to have a dream, having relentless commitment to realising that dream and being constantly positive and focused on where we could be.

I think good manners, courtesy and respectfulness towards others has also helped carry me along the way, also my absolute refusal to allow myself to fail. Most importantly, I have always hired the best people; in many cases, people who are smarter and brighter than me. Then I have created an environment in which they could excel.

Christine Booth is rigorous in her approach to business.

I have a target of 27 million pounds, 300 full- and 100 part-time staff and I have to make a 43 per cent contribution. My tip is to have a vision of where you are going, a three- to five-year goal and be disciplined in everything you do to achieve that. The vision is my framework, my bottom line is discipline. I haven't a clue how I got here, but it all seems to work. I am not autocratic in management, but I have high expectations of everyone. Of course, everyone wants to work in a successful business and my job is to ensure this happens, so my staff love their jobs.

Keep the Faith

Believe in yourself, the people around you and the product or service you are associated with. That belief is infectious and soon it will spread among clients, assuring you of a secure future. Hannah Evans agrees: 'Do something you really believe in, enjoy it and do it the way you want to do it. This way all the hard work doesn't feel like an uphill struggle. I also think you need to be leading the market, not following it. That way you are always ahead of the competition. Keep an eye on market trends and be quick to react. Above all, have integrity.'

Above and beyond the workaday challenges of watching company finances and employing brilliant people, one anonymous contributor believes faith and focus will help when it comes to achieving goals. 'Always look forward to a shared goal. Hang in there when times are tough. Every problem will have a solution. Be positive and upbeat because your attitude sets the culture of the organisation. Try to avoid politics so everyone can concentrate on the work they are employed to do. The workplace should be enjoyable and focused, then people will want to give their best.'

Focus

Sometimes work runs rampant through all areas of your life. That's not necessarily an asset but it is understandable if your business becomes your focus, and in stalking success focus is a virtue and one that comes without an 'off' switch.

Natalie Douglas sums up her rise to the boardroom like this: 'Bloody hard work . . . It's very difficult as a woman because we have other things we have to do, but keep focused and stay determined. Understand there will be good and bad days. Be careful who you trust, but when you get someone who is good, keep them safe. Trust your heart.'

Successful enterprises can be risky businesses. It may be that Deborah Adshead is stating the obvious when she points out the need for a good network of potential customers. She adds:

Financial stability helps, but then again I started with no money and if I had waited until I had some, I would never have started. Be determined, see a goal and don't be scared. I wanted excitement, variety and control. When I worked full-time for someone else I had loads of money but was unhappy. Now I have less money, but I'm getting fulfilment from doing it all myself – everything from painting the offices to getting new customers. It's all mine. Passion is what you need to succeed. Sixteen-hour days are inevitable in the early days. If you don't love what you are doing you won't survive.

Survive to Thrive

With success comes stress, often in bucket loads. There's little point in carving a stunning career if you are left a wobbling wreck. It's vital to find coping techniques. When it comes to surviving stress at the top Kate Ancketill has mastered the art of self-hypnosis. 'I was grinding my teeth in my sleep, without realising what I was doing. I cracked the enamel of perfectly healthy teeth. It was very annoying and very expensive. Obviously it was something in my subconscious.' To find answers she went to a hypnotherapist and, on her first visit, was taught the skill of self-hypnosis.

I can put myself to sleep anywhere. I never slept on a plane until I learned how to do this and, as I travel for four months of the year, it has been a huge bonus. Self-hypnosis helps with the way you perceive problems. They don't become overwhelming and you have a much greater perspective. It is fantastic for managing stress and controlling the fight and flight response. Nothing bothers me really. I may find stuff exasperating but it would be impossible for work to make me stressed now.

The Best of the Rest

When it came to sharing tips for the top, the women I interviewed revealed their individuality. Here is a wide-ranging selection of advice from women who made their own way up the slopes of success.

Fiona Cruickshank has a short, sharp recipe for creating a successful enterprise: 'Hard work, a bit of luck, the right product or service and an absolute conviction it is going to work.'

Jeanette Sargent, a jewellery maker, has one straightforward business tip that's so fundamental it may well fall under the radar: 'Just ask. If you really want to do some work for a particular company or individual – ask them. The worst they can say is no and you're no worse off than you were before you asked. If your experience is anything like mine, many will say yes. I asked Ruth Badger, finalist in the BBC show *The Apprentice* if I could make a necklace for her and she agreed!'

Fiona Sheridan favours taking an overview. 'Be clear on what your strategic focus is. Know what your must-dos are and don't be sidetracked. Also have a great and inspired team around you and, if things go wrong, be strong.' While Justine Dignam, looking at it from a different angle, believes you should pay people to do the things you don't want to do.

Some people have short, sharp wise words to impart. For Dianne Sharp the key word is passion while Alison Boxall says determination is all important. Involving other people, especially family members, in decision making can make the boardroom a less lonely place. Nicole Paradise agrees, 'Keep it simple. Stick to what you are good at.'

Yvonne Lumley has two valuable pieces of advice for women in business. 'The rules of business are still being set by men. Learn to be competitive as a woman – which means unlearning what we were taught as girls. And put regular small amounts of effort in the business rather than peaking and troughing.' Anita Brough looks at it this way: 'Never miss a good public-relations opportunity. Always be professional and manage your image.' The broad-ranging demands of good business management are summed up by one female entrepreneur: 'Transparent hierarchy, honesty, having a motivated and committed team, having fun and fulfilling the psychological needs of both employees and customers. Focus on excellent customer service. No customers, no business!' Tracy Viner, revealing something of the cauldron behind the veneer of most businesswomen, says: 'I started my own company because I knew it was now or never and I have devised it as much as I could to give me flexibility . . . but I still fear I will be found out.' And, finally, remember Alison Kennedy's simple but essential advice: 'Don't give up.'

The fear of being found out is always there but it can be overcome. One great antidote to it is the pure, unalloyed joy a roaring business can bring. It's not all about the money – although that helps. It's the personal investment that pays the real dividends, one that doesn't show itself on a balance sheet. That's the motivation for women like those featured in this book who get up horribly early, put in untold hours at their desks and sacrifice slices of life that many people take for granted. That and the excitement that pulses through a life in business. At the end of all my research perhaps my favourite piece of advice comes from Sonita Alleyne who told me: 'Business is like being in a playground looking for the next exciting adventure.'

Top Tips

■ never undersell yourself

■ buy the best clothes you can afford

■ smile

■ for both your business and personal life keep lists of:
   – things to do
   – people's birthdays
   – special notes

■ look after yourself:
   – have a regular good haircut
   – look well groomed

■ have a private life and keep it private

■ expect people to let you down

■ give lots of genuine praise

■ never stop learning

■ take a break
   – long or short but take time out

- tell your children how wonderful they are – all the time, even if they aren't being particularly wonderful

- know when to talk and when to stay quiet

- take calculated risks

- don't be afraid to be different

- whatever it is you want to do, try it

- never let anyone be bullied and don't bully others

- if you are going to lie, be consistent

- go that extra ten miles for your clients – they will always remember

- don't let anyone walk over you

- always say thank you and mean it

- learn how to deliver a great presentation in public

- know when to move on and never go back

- read extensively

■ speak coherently and articulate properly

■ if you have got it, flaunt it (in moderation!)

■ learn to let go of:
  – anger
  – bad memories
  – blame
  – jealousy

■ promote yourself

■ don't be afraid to ask for help

■ always attempt to overdeliver

■ ask people to recommend you (and reciprocate)

■ buy domestic help as soon as you can

■ build a small select network of very special friends

■ don't miss important personal events for the sake of your career

■ get a good trustworthy financial adviser for you and your business as soon as possible

- follow up and follow through

- don't take everything seriously, learn to laugh at yourself and others

- trust people until they show you otherwise then never go there again!

- get plenty of sleep

- always have a plan B or even a plan C!

- avoid mixing business and friendship or at least recognise a different type of friendship

- always aim for the top

- never ever ever give up

- arrive on time and leave before the end

- prepare before you go to meetings

- take a course on influencing and selling skills

- keep up to date with technology

- get a fantastic PA and do everything to make him or her happy

- when your children are little, start a present drawer and keep things available for gifts, for parties, etc., buy birthday cards and gift wrap in bulk

- have a birthday calendar and buy and wrap in advance

- always have a personal activity planned in advance to look forward to

- say 'yes I can' and worry later if you can't

- eliminate negative people in your life

- forgive but never forget!

'Don'ts'

- do the opposite of the previous list

- cry

- whinge

- wimp

- try and look like the men

- be a swot

- show off

- gamble the family fortune

- be a wallflower

- be rude

- ignore people just because you don't think they can't help you

- buy friendship – either business or personal

- compromise your personal principles

- have bad table manners or eating habits

- blame other people

- be a bitch

- be a prude

- swear or use profanities

- be pigeon-holed

- dash other people's dreams

- take credit for work you have not originated

- live on credit

- let anyone else run your financial affairs

- oversell

- have false modesty

- patronise

- be a bad loser

- be a brown nose

- be a smart arse

- pretend to like sporting activities if you really hate them

- be sycophantic

- pretend you know something if you really have no idea

- condemn without the facts

- be miserly

- be ruthless

- be uncharitable

- lack focus

- preach

- be callous

- ambush people

- belittle people

■ take your anger out on those people who love you (and if you do, say sorry)

■ leave important matters to chance

■ overreact

■ be superficial

■ be egotistical

■ be a pushover

■ and, finally, don't do what I do because I don't do it right all the time!

Resources

United Kingdom

The Institute of Directors (IoD)

www.iod.com

116 Pall Mall, London SW1Y 5ED

0207 839 1233

With a worldwide membership, the IoD provides a professional network that reaches into every corner of the business community. Membership spans a whole spectrum of business leadership, from the largest public companies to the smallest private firms. Members receive benefits including advice, training, conference and publications. The IoD represents its members' concerns to the government and provides professional business support wherever needed.

Vistage International (Previously TEC International)

www.vistage.com

UK office: One Crown Walk, Jewry Street, Winchester,

Hampshire SO23 8BD

01962 841 188

Vistage International helps companies outperform the competition. Business leaders come to Vistage to accelerate the growth of their business and of themselves. Growth comes from one-to-one executive coaching, access to a group of trusted peers and entry into the world-wide network of more than 10,000 executives.

The Academy for Chief Executives

www.chiefexecutive.com

Main office: Wisdom House, 4 Brockley Close, Stanmore, Middx HA7 4QL

0870 228 3369

The aim of the academy is to create a community of business leaders who are willing to share their experiences, and through trust and support help each other achieve extraordinary things. Back in 1996, the academy started with just two groups and 23 members. Today it has a membership of over 400 business leaders from across the UK.

Companies House

www.companieshouse.gov.uk

Main office: Crown Way, Maindy, Cardiff CF14 3UZ

Contact Centre: 0870 3333 636

The main functions of Companies House include incorporating and dissolving limited companies, examining and storing company information and making all this information available to the public. The site also gives a lot of useful information with regards to running a company.

Chamber Awards

www.chamberawards.co.uk

See p. 149 for more information.

First Women Awards

www.firstwomenawards.co.uk

See p. 148 for more information.

Prowess Awards

www.prowess.org.uk

See p. 150 for more information.

Women4Business Awards

www.women4business.co.uk

See p. 149 for more information.

www.linkedin.com

LinkedIn strengthens and extends your existing network of trusted contacts and is a networking tool that helps you discover inside connections.

www.bosstoboss.com

Boss to Boss online business network and management forum, with business support tools and personal development.

www.myspace.com/www.facebook.com

Meet people from your area and keep in touch. Includes blog, forums, email, groups, games and events.

Republic of Ireland

LIFT Development Partnership

www.lift.ie

31/32 Parnell Square, Dublin 1, Ireland

+353 1 8897 766

The Trade Union movement has been to the fore in achieving real improvements for women. However – like many organisations – unions have a deficit of women in leadership roles. The LIFT Development partnership of the Irish Congress of Trade Unions (ICTU), the Institute of Public Administration (IPA) and the National Centre for Partnership and Performance (NCPP) was formed to develop strategies which promote the inclusion of women across all levels of trade union hierarchies and ensure their participation at every level of union organisation with particular emphasis on the identification, development and support of future women leaders.

Companies Registration Office

www.cro.ie

Parnell House, 14 Parnell Square, Dublin 1

+353 1 804 5200

The Companies Registration Office is the central repository of public statutory information on Irish companies. The CRO operates under the aegis of the Department of Enterprise Trade and Employment. The CRO is the statutory authority for registering new companies in the Republic of Ireland and registering business names.

Chambers of Commerce of Ireland

www.chambers.ie

7 Clare Street, Dublin 2

+353 1 644 7200

The mission of Chambers Ireland is to represent the business interests of the member companies, to promote the competitiveness of business in Ireland and to enable the development of the chamber network in Ireland. Chambers Ireland offers support, assistance and training to help local chambers grow and provide the best service possible to their member companies. It acts as guardian of the chamber brand in Ireland and operates the chamber quality accreditation process. It also negotiates commercial agreements and develops national public relations and marketing campaigns on behalf of the national network.

Women Mean Business Conference & Awards

www.womenmeanbusiness.com/awards

47 Harrington Street, Dublin 8, Ireland

+353 1 4155 056

Women really are blazing new trails across Irish business, whether as entrepreneurs or as corporate leaders. In areas as diverse as science, technology, tourism, business services and manufacturing, Irish businesses are benefiting from the fresh ideas, dedication, and leadership that women can bring. The Women Mean Business Awards recognise their achievements to encourage even more women to succeed in their chosen field, and give budding entrepreneurs the impetus they need to start their own business.

South Africa

Women in Business

www.womeninbusiness.org.za

033 267 7028

From humble beginnings Women In Business has established itself as an organisation of distinction. Initiated in June 2005, the forum was established out of a need for women to give and receive knowledge, skills, support, and friendship. It runs courses, networking events and also a mentor programme.

Inspiring Women

www.inspiringwomen.co.za

PO Box 55062, Sunset Beach, South Africa, 7441

+27 84 361 3606

The South African Professional and Businesswomen's Network provides business, financial and personal education, inspiration and motivation for women across South Africa and facilitates opportunities for them to network, learn and be inspired by role models, mentorship and by each other.

Women's Network

www.womensnet.co.za

PO Box 662, Brackenfell, Western Cape, South Africa, 7561

This website provides general advice and information for businesswomen in South Africa.

South African Chamber of Business

www.sacob.co.za

PO Box 213, Saxonwold, 2132

+27 11 446 3800

SACOB is the largest business organisation in South Africa. Through its constituent chambers, it has a total membership of close to 20,000 businesses, most of them small and medium-sized. Some 80 of the largest business corporations in South Africa are direct members of SACOB, while nearly 20 national associations are affiliated members. These associations represent the interests of specific sectors of the economy.

Australia

The Freehills Women in Business Network

www.freehills.com.au

MLC Centre, 19 Martin Place, Sydney NSW 2000,

GPO Box 4227, Sydney NSW 2001

+61 2 9225 5000

The Freehills Women in Business networking forum was established in 1994 and represents industries as diverse as banking, telecommunications, retail, publishing, government, law and the judiciary. Women in Business aims to foster networks among women at all stages in their professional careers, by providing opportunities for senior businesswomen from diverse organisations and industries to meet one another and exchange views and experiences, as well as a comfortable environment for women who are up and coming in their field to meet senior women in business.

NSW Small Business

Women in Business Mentor Programme

www.smallbiz.nsw.gov.au

NSW Department of State and Regional Development,

GPO Box 5477, Sydney NSW 2001

+1300 134 359

The Women in Business Mentor Programme helps up-and-coming women business owners (mentorees) grow their business by linking them with experienced business people (mentors). The programme, which encourages co-operative learning between business people, uses mentoring, practical sessions and networking to help women improve their business skills and boost their confidence.

Women's Network Australia

www.womensnetwork.com.au

PO Box 1723, Sunnybank Hills, QLD Australia 4109

+ 61 7 3272 8222

Women's Network Australia is Australia's leading membership-based network for business and professional women. WNA provides an extensive range of benefits and services all aimed at enhancing the professional and personal lives of businesswomen across Australia. For nearly two decades Women's Network Australia has been empowering and encouraging women in their quest for business and career success and is now positioned as the leading networking organisation for business and professional women in Australia.

Australian Chamber of Commerce and Industry

www.acci.asn.au

Commerce House, Level 3, 24 Brisbane Avenue, Barton Act 2600

+61 2 6273 2311

The Australian Chamber of Commerce and Industry (ACCI) is one of Australia's enduring institutions. The role of ACCI is to represent the interests of business at a national level as well as internationally. Through its network of businesses, each ACCI member organisation identifies the concerns of its members and plans united action. In this way business policies are developed and strategies for change are implemented. ACCI operates at a national and international level, making sure the concerns of business are represented to government at the federal level, and to the community at large.

qbr Women in Business Awards

www.qbr.com.au/wib

Publishing Services Australia, PO Box 312, Fortitude Valley,
QLD Australia 4000

+07 3854 1286

The inaugural 2006 Women in Business Awards provided formal recognition of the achievements of Queensland's businesswomen and the increasingly important role they are playing in the community. The Women in Business Awards recognise leading businesswomen across key industry categories from agriculture to tourism & hospitality.

New Zealand

Her Business Network

www.herbusinessmagazine.com

Stretton Publishing Company Ltd, Corner of Thames and Marshall Streets, PO Box 65, Morrinsville 3340, New Zealand

+07 889 4053

Her Business magazine is the national sponsor, coordinator and administrator of the Her Business Networks throughout New Zealand. Meetings are informal, with networking, socialising, trading, mentoring and relaxing being the key ingredients. Successful role models educate and enlighten by speaking about their experiences and this is an empowering format facilitated part-time by Her Business Network Coordinators who operate their own successful businesses in the community.

Ministry of Women's Affairs

www.mwa.govt.nz

Level 2, Rivera Building, 48 Mulgrave Street, Thorndon, Willington, PO Box 10 049, New Zealand

+04 915 7112

Ministry of Women's Affairs is the New Zealand government's source of advice on ways to improve the lives of women. It provides advice on policy solutions to improve the status of women, recommends suitable women nominees for state sector boards and manages New Zealand's international obligations in relation to the status of women, in particular under the United Nations Convention for the Elimination of Discrimination Against Women.

Business Mentors New Zealand

www.businessmentor.org.nz

National Office, PO Box 9043, Newmarket, Auckland 1149, New Zealand

+0800 103400

This national mentoring service is now called Business Mentors New Zealand (BMNZ). This organisation provides a national mentor network to help any New Zealand company which has been in business for at least 12 months and has less than 25 employees.

Business & Professional Women (BPW)

www.bpwnz.org.nz

PO Box 28-326, Remuera, Auckland 1136, New Zealand

BPW NZ aims to improve the position of women in business, trade, and the professions and in the economic life of their countries. They promote worldwide friendship, cooperation and understanding between business and professional women, and collect and present the views of business and professional women to parliament, as well as to national and international organisations and agencies.

New Zealand Companies Office

www.companies.govt.nz

Northern Business Centre, Private Bag 92061, Auckland Mail Centre, Auckland 1142, New Zealand

+64 3 9622602

The Companies Office is the government agency responsible for the administration of corporate body registers, including the Companies Register. It offers a range of online services that are convenient, fast and simple – saving time and money. Online services include forming a company, obtaining a company tax number and maintaining company details.

New Zealand Chamber of Commerce

www.nzchamber.co.nz

11 Mayoral Drive, PO Box 47, Auckland, New Zealand

+09 309 3100

Index

3i 96
4C Change Limited 80

Ab Fab Charity Fashion Show 195
Academy of Chief Executives (ACE)
    133, 134
accessories 96–7
accounts 17, 201
accreditation 130–1
active listening 55
Admirable Crichton, The 40–1
Adshead, Deborah 49, 58, 95, 142,
    170, 178, 205–6
Ahmadi, Pooya 41, 45, 56, 83–4, 99,
    143, 171, 182
alcohol 71, 112, 116
Alleyne, Sonita 77, 104, 135, 208
ambition 6, 68, 203–4
AMEC plc 27, 115
anally-retentive qualities 18, 19
Ancketill, Kate 25, 38–9, 98, 131, 180,
    206
appearance, importance of your
    99–100
    see also dress codes
Apprentice, The (TV show) 207
Astaire, Fred 87

Astor, Nancy 45, 173
auditors 17
authority 33
awards 147–51

Badger, Ruth 207
Balding, Clare 25, 98, 143, 174
bank managers 27
Bannister, Victoria 42, 135, 179, 188
Barr, Roseanne 31, 57
barriers to entry 9–44
battles, choosing carefully 30
BBC see British Broadcasting
    Corporation
belittling people 20
birthdays 73
black-tie events 102
Blair, Tony 91
bloopers 192–3
board of directors, exclusive male 6
body language 164–5
Bombeck, Erma 57
Booth, Christine 2, 46, 58, 106, 182,
    204
Bounds, Deirdre 58, 88, 104, 142, 170
Boxall, Alison 58, 98–9, 174, 207
bragging 145–6

brands
  creation 201
  promotion 147
breakdowns 43, 60
British Broadcasting Corporation
  (BBC) 25, 207
Brough, Anita 76, 104, 182, 207
Brown, Bonnie 65–6
Brown, Sandra 46, 143, 158, 195–7
bullying 21
Burgess, Justine 24–5
burn out 58
business cards 118, 120
Business Channel 56
business failure 192, 200
Business Links 132, 148
business support 198–9
  see also expert advice; mentors

Cabinet Office 50
Cabinet Office Management 115–16
Camden Electronics Limited 80
career crises 130
career paths 12–16
career progression 130–1, 139
caring for others 59–64
Carter, Gail 2, 49, 78–9, 96, 126, 142,
  174
case studies
  enterprise creation 193–7
  overcoming hurdles 35–41
  work-life balance 62–4
catering companies 40–1
Catling, Sue 81, 91, 112, 134, 154, 168,
  182, 202
CBI (Confederation of British
  Industry) 148

challenges 10
Chamber of Commerce 136, 148, 193
  Regional Awards 149
Chanel, Coco 89–90, 99
Chartered Institute of Personnel and
  Development 70–1
chauvinism 11
cheques, company 33–4
choice 83
Churchill, Winston 157
City Women's Network 24
clarification, asking for 20
cleavage 98, 99
Cleveland, Alexis 2, 50, 58, 115–16,
  126
clothing see dress codes
clubs 120
co-ownership 200
coaching, work/life balance 70–1, 85
codes of conduct 169
Collins, Denise 2, 28, 96, 111, 153,
  174
Common Purpose 132–3
company cheques 33–4
competitions 147–8
compromise 21, 53–5
Confederation of British Industry
  (CBI) 148
confidence 5, 43, 152
confrontations 52–3
Conley, Rosemary 49, 73–4, 90, 126,
  152–3, 170
Conservative Party 81, 91, 134
construction 27
Construction Speciality UK Limited
  135
contacts see networking

continuing professional development (CPD) 129–30
contracts 17, 33
control freaks 72
conversation pieces 114–15
Cosmopolitan magazine 194
cot death 36–7
Courtney, Polly 23–4
Cowley, Lesley 42, 83, 88, 135, 142, 202
Crawford, Tom 121–2
cricket 108
Cruickshank, Fiona 27, 50, 97, 116, 169, 188, 207
CV (curriculum vitae) 151

Davies, Linda 68–9
Day, Sue 66
deadlines 19
Deaves, Sarah 49, 76, 113–14, 153, 182, 202
defensive manoeuvres 18–21
degrees 5, 13
delegation 72, 81
Deloitte 121–2
Dennison, Helena 24
designer clothes 97
determination 202
Devonshire Quarter Traders Association 195
diary keeping 20
Dignam, Justine 81, 88, 104, 174, 207
directors
  liabilities 16–17
  non-executive 200
  of owner-managed companies 15
  of public limited companies 15–16
  responsibilities 16–17
  unequal pay 6–7
  see also board of directors
discrimination 21–30, 67–8
Disney-ABC Television 177
divorce 62–4
Doherty, Jayne 2, 25, 53, 58
domestic chores 57, 58
domestic help 69–70, 74, 83, 85
  see also nannies
Douglas, Natalie 74, 97, 111, 134, 152, 181, 205
dress codes 87–102
  accessories 96–7
  black-tie events 102
  blending in 92
  choosing colours 90, 95–6
  cleavage 98, 99
  conservative 95
  designer clothes 97
  dressing down 91
  faux pas 93–4, 98
  glamour 92
  importance of appearance 99–100
  jewellery 96
  personal shoppers 101
  scrutiny 97–8
  shoes 100, 101
  survival guide 100–2
  wardrobe mishaps 93
Duckham, Wendy 10, 115, 135, 169, 183, 202–3
dyslexia 127

Earl, Belinda 166
education 5, 13, 125–40
  and career crises 130

and career progression 130–1, 139
government initiatives 132–4
grants for 133, 139
online 132–3
survival guide 139–40
email 162–3, 171
emotional control 20
emotional intelligence 134–5
empathy 117
employment law 17, 67–9
employment tribunals 30
Enos, Laurianne 2, 135, 153
enterprise creation 186–217
and ambition 203–4
building businesses 197–8
case examples 193–7
coping with stress 206
don'ts 214–17
and focus 205–6
and self-belief 204–5
and staff 202–4
successful 198
support for 198–9
survival guide 199–201
time issues 191
tips 2, 188–9, 201–2, 206–8, 209–13
Equal Opportunities Commission
24, 30
Equal Pay Act 1970 24
equality 183–4
Ernst & Young, Risk Advisory
Services 27, 134
erotica 194–5
Evans, Hannah 78, 88, 115, 126, 142,
169, 204
evening classes 120
Everywoman Award 149

experience 125–6
expert advice 30
eye contact 142

Facebook 121
faux pas 93–4, 98, 192–3
feminine qualities, preservation 3
feminine wiles 180–1
filing 13
finance, raising 41
Finland 5
Finnegan, Judy 93
First Choice Select Limited 80, 129
First Woman Award 148
flexible working 66
football 106, 109, 110
Ford 28
foreign languages 135
France 7
franchisees 199
Frewen, Rolline 2, 40–1, 76, 88, 126,
142, 153
friends, working for 179–80
Friends Reunited 77
FTSE 100 companies 5, 6

Gannon, Justine 82, 88, 104, 174, 207
Gartside, Alexander 196
Gash, Julia 88, 113, 194–5, 197
Gash UK Ltd 194–5
GDR Creative Intelligence 38–9
genuineness 118
Germany 7
getting noticed see self-promotion
glamour 92
golf 106, 107
Google 65–6, 67

gossip 158, 159, 166–70, 171
government initiatives 132–4
grants 133, 139
Great Western Hotels GB 91–2
Green, Diana 43, 84, 98–9, 183
Grimke, Sarah Moore 21
grudges 19
Guardian (newspaper) 6–7, 24
guilt 22, 58, 60–1, 70–1, 76, 83, 85
Guise, Dr Jane 10, 53, 58, 169,
    182, 188
gyms 107–8

Hague, William 193
haircuts 101
Harvey, Barbara 2, 58, 81–2, 142, 168,
    181
`having it all' 82–3
Health and Case Management
    Limited 50–1
health and safety 17
help, asking for 71, 72
    see also domestic help
Hinxman, Lynda 90, 115, 143
Hiya 35–8
Hobsbawm, Julia 70
holidays 73, 79–80, 86
homemaking 59–64
horse racing 108–9
house husbands 6, 74
housekeepers 69
Howard, Gillian 68
Hughes, Angela 53, 80–1, 131, 135–6,
    188
humour 21
husbands 192
    see also house husbands

i-to-i 170
ideas, stealing *see* plagiarism
IDIS Limited 97, 181
Image Source Limited 82
indemnity insurance 34
Industry Training Boards 132
innovation 202
insecurity 32
insolvency, trading during 16
Institute of Directors (IoD) 33, 133,
    136, 148, 193–4
Regional and National Director
    Awards 149
Institute of Mechanical Engineers 95
interest, showing 113–14, 117
Internet
and education 132–3
and food shopping 72
and networking 120, 121
interviews 99
investment banking 23–4, 25, 67–8
Italy 5, 91
Izziwizzikids 98–9

Jaegar 166
JD Approach 95
jealousy 176, 180
jewellery 96
job security 42
Joyce Estate Agents 53
JVL Products Limited 53, 80–1, 131

Kay, Karen 91–2
Kay, Nicola 80, 97–8, 104, 142, 158,
    174
Kennedy, Alison 10, 80, 104, 208
Kenny, Julie 2, 62–4, 142, 178

Kingsley, Joy 2, 88, 153, 176, 181
KPMG 66

law 128
Leading Women/People Factors 114
legal battles 67–8
Leschen, Caryn 187
liabilities, directors' 16–17
lies, white 160, 163–5, 210
Lilani, Pinky 10, 76, 114, 188
limits, understanding your 81–2,
    86
linkedin.com 120
list writing 72–3, 85, 209
listening, active 55
'little wins' 55
Lockwood, Anne 41–2, 80, 111–12,
    129, 170, 174
London School of Economics 77
losing face 52
Lumley, Yvonne 10, 88, 114, 142, 174,
    207

MacDonald, Heather 43, 53, 90,
    134–5, 183, 188
Madeley, Richard 93
male domination 3–4, 5–6, 27
    see also discrimination
management buyouts 14
Management Today magazine 178
managing women 173–85
    and feminine wiles 180–1
    and office equality 183–4
    survival guide 185
    tips 174, 182–3
manicures 101
Mannes, Marya 59

Master of Business Administration
    (MBA) 136–7
maternity leave 5
Mechetronics Limited 168
media 151–2
Media Management Group 82
meetings 19–21, 27
Members of Parliament (MPs) 91
memory 115
men
    domination 3–4, 5–6, 27
    home lives 60–2
    and sexual discrimination 21–30,
        67–8
    see also house husbands; husbands
mentors 14, 15, 137–8
Merfield, Helen 50–1, 58, 79–80, 114,
    138, 143, 170, 188
Moir, Julia 88, 104, 126, 142, 174
Moira Anderson Foundation 195–7
motherhood 22, 36–8, 42
multi-tasking 60
Murphy, Maureen 32
My Space 121

Nabarro 28
nannies 63, 69
'need to be liked' 31–2
networking
    alternatives to 119–20
    through classes and clubs 120
    conversation pieces for 114–15
    follow ups 115–16, 118
    grouping contacts 122
    Internet 120, 121
    maintaining contacts 121–3
    moving on tips 118

referrals 120
and smiling 117
survival guide 117–19
targets 114, 118
Nominet UK 83
non-executive directors 200
note keeping 20

Observer (newspaper) 24, 177, 194
office grapevine, using to your
advantage 52
Office of National Statistics 6
office politics 157–72
and email 162–3, 171
gossip 158, 159, 166–70, 171
and plagiarism 50–1
survival guide 170–1
tips for dealing with 158, 161–2
white lies 160, 163–5
openness, unwise 32–3, 34–5
opportunity, women's exclusion from
5–6
over weight 99
see also weight loss
overcompensation 32

paedophilia 195–7
Pankhurst, Julie 77
Pankhurst, Steve 77
Pannone LLP 176
Paradise, Nicole 28, 58, 116, 142, 189,
207
paraphrasing 55
parenting 36–7, 58–64, 66–7, 69–70,
73–85, 179, 210, 213
see also nannies
partnerships 200

party-design companies 40–1
Pattinson, Nicky 35–8, 84, 97, 158,
182, 189
pay gap 6–7, 24
pedicures 101
peer support 30
perfectionism 75, 81–2
personal shoppers 101
personal strengths 18–19
personal tragedy 36–8
personal weaknesses 18–19, 29
pharmaceutical industry 27
Piccalilly 78, 115
plagiarism 20, 46–56
compromise regarding 53–5
confrontation regarding 52–3
remaining silent about 54
survival guide 51
Plato 157
politicians 32, 50, 81, 91, 164, 177–8
popularity contests 31–2
positivity 84
Potential Plus 197
power 31–2
praise 183, 185
prescription medication 71
press 151–2
prioritising 58, 82–4
promotion, being passed over 25
proving yourself 43
Prowess Awards 150
Psychologies magazine 187
public limited companies 15–16
public relations (PR) opportunities
151
public sector 53
public speaking events 119–20, 133

Pyronix Limited 62–4, 178
Ratner, Gerald 33
recognition 47–8
referrals 120
relatives, ageing 62
relaxation 58
responsibilities, directors' 16–17
retail trends analysis 38–9
revenge, waiting for the right
   moment 29
rights, employment 67–9
Rivers, Joan 103
Rodin, Auguste 125
Rogers, Ginger 87
Roosevelt, Eleanor 2
Roxbrough, Johnny 40
Royal Bath & West of England Society
   53
Russel Richardson & Sons Limited 182

S & A Foods 75, 201–2
sacrifice 83
sales 37–8
   propositions 200
Salford University 80
Sargent, Jeanette 42, 58, 96, 114, 168,
   174, 207
Scandrett, Barbara 88, 112, 142, 158,
   188
scepticism 2
Schmidt, Eric 65
Scotsman (newspaper) 196–7
self-belief 42, 204–5
self-care 209
self-employment
   and parenting 77–9
   see also enterprise creation

self-hypnosis 206
self-promotion 141–55
   survival guide 154–5
   tips 142–3, 152–4
sex industry 194–5
sexism 21–30, 67–8
Sexual Discrimination Act (1975) 24
sexual harassment 24–5, 27
Sharp, Dianne 49–50, 143, 168, 188,
   189, 207
Sharpe, Fay 53, 79, 104, 183
Sheffield Hallam University 81–2, 84,
   90, 106
Sheridan, Fiona 27, 79, 96, 134, 158,
   183, 207
shoes 100, 101
silence, maintaining 54
Sinatra, Frank 199
smiling 117, 142
Smith, Jacqui 177–8
social networking sites 121
Sofer, Rabbi 71
Somethin' Else 77
Specials Laboratory Limited 97
Spellman, Ruth 10, 95, 136, 143, 188
Spice Magic 114
sport 103, 105–10, 119
   spectating 108–9
sports gear 42
sports presenters 25
Sportsshoes Unlimited 135
staff 202–4
   see also managing women
standing down 21
start-ups see enterprise creation
Stewart, Mary 141
Stokvis Tapes 202

stomach stapling 63–4
strategic overviews 207
stress management 206
stubbornness 21
Sunday Times, The (newspaper) 68–9
support 31, 42, 192
  unwise sources of 56
  see also business support
survival guides 18–21
  discrimination 28–30
  dress codes 100–2
  education 139–40
  enterprise creation 199–201
  managing women 185
  networking 117–19
  office politics 170–1
  plagiarism 51
  self-promotion 154–5
  work/life balance 85–6
Sweeney, Anne 177
SWOT analysis 18–19

tennis 108
thank yous 119
Thatcher, Margaret 91, 177
Thaves, Bob 87
time issues 79–80, 191
Times, The (newspaper) 66, 70, 122
to do lists 72–3, 85
trainers 129
Training and Enterprise Councils 132
TV presenters 25, 98

undervaluing yourself 29
United States 5, 70–1

values 201–2
Vanstone, Fiona 27, 58, 98–9, 115, 143, 188
Vaughan, Christina 2, 10, 82–3, 88, 104, 126, 168–9, 174, 203–4
Viner, Tracy 43, 49, 81, 96, 115, 153, 181–2, 188, 208
vision 201–2
Vistage 133–4

Wakefield College 53, 90
wardrobes *see* dress codes
Warsi, Perween 75, 88, 104, 126, 142, 174, 201–2
wealth 192
weekends 58
weight loss 63–4
West, Mae 173
Whitton, Charlotte 9
Women4Business 149–50
Women & Technology Awards 150–1
Women in Ethical Businesses Award (WEBA) 150
work/life balance 57–86
  coaching for 70–1, 85
  prioritising work 82–4
  and self-employment 77–9
  survival guide for 85–6
  and time management 79–81
  tips 58, 71–6, 85–6
working hours 79–80
Worrall, Ann 10, 112, 143, 182–3, 202
Wyse, Lois 18

Zibrant 53

KITCHEN TABLE TYCOON

How to make it work as a mother and an entrepreneur

by Anita Naik

Become a successful business woman from home

Are you eager to combine the roles of mother and entrepreneur but wondering how to get started? If so, you are not alone. Many mothers are quitting their day jobs and starting up on their own, eager to cut out the nursery fees and see more of their kids. If that sounds like your dream, writer Anita Naik can help you make it come true. Having worked from home for 16 successful years, she can give you the true, nitty-gritty details on what it really means to start and run your business from your kitchen table, including:

- How to find out if you're suited to working on your own
- How to discover your 'big business idea'
- How to get your business off the ground
- How to make your business successful
- How to deal with mummy versus work guilt
- How to juggle family, work and YOU time
- And where to go for support, help and advice

Kitchen Table Tycoon also shows you how to create and research a realistic business idea, how to find your start-up costs, and how to navigate your way through the ups and downs of running your own business.

With inspiring stories and advice from successful entrepreneurial mothers who have been there and done that, *Kitchen Table Tycoon* can show even the most nervous of mumpreneurs how it's more than possible to have to have a great business and a great life.

ISBN: 978 0 7499 2791 2

ASK FOR IT

How women can get what they really want – at work and at home

by Linda Babcock and Sara Laschever

If you're a woman, you probably have a voice inside your head that says: 'Don't get pushy . . . Don't you have enough already? Why can't you be happy with what you've got?' The time has come to talk back to that voice . . .

To research this groundbreaking book, Linda Babcock and Sara Laschever spent several years talking to thousands of women about the high cost of failing to ask for what they want. Through that research, one thing became abundantly clear: feelings of self-doubt consistently prevent women from getting the things they desire most, whether it's a pay rise, a nicer office, or even just some help around the house.

In *Ask for It*, the authors have developed a unique, cooperative approach to negotiating that begins before you ever get to a bargaining table, one that will help women realise their self-worth and identify their goals as well as maximise their bargaining power and manage emotions on both sides. It will help propel you to new places both professionally and personally – and open doors you thought were closed.

Essential reading for women everywhere, *Ask for It* will help you recognise how much more you deserve – and show you how to get it.

ISBN: 978 0 7499 2935 0

BUYING AND SELLING A BUSINESS

An entrepreneurs guide

by Jo Haigh

An essential guide to trading businesses from an expert in the field

For many the dream of owning their own business remains just that – even if you have a great idea, the work and money involved in building a business from the ground up can prove too daunting. What few aspiring entrepreneurs realise is that buying an existing business can be far easier to accomplish, sometimes with little or no money at all, and can be just as satisfying a route to self-sufficiency.

Expert corporate financier Jo Haigh takes you through the entire process, from identifying your target business and assembling the right team to support you, to valuation, agreeing terms and finding the necessary finance. She helps you ensure your deal is the right deal for you, offering advice on running the business you buy and implementing proper exit strategies from the start. With valuable appendices containing typical documentation (letters of intent, confidentiality agreements, etc.), this book is a one-stop resource to closing the deal – and transforming your life.

ISBN: 978 0 7499 2839 1

THE BUSINESS RULES

Protect yourself and your company from over 100 hidden pitfalls

by Jo Haigh

Information that every company owner, director or sole trader needs to know

Did you know that, if you're a director of a company, liquidators can bring actions against you personally? Or that, if your employee commits an offence, you may also have to compensate the victim – even if the criminal action is only incidentally related to the employee's duties?

The world of business is filled with opportunities, but also rife with legal pitfalls such as these. *The Business Rules* helps small business owners and managers recognise and avoid over 100 hazards that can damage – and in some cases ruin – your company. An accessible, one-stop resource, Jo Haigh's book covers all areas of your company, from structure and funding to compliance and accounting, and helps any director or manager navigate the challenges of the business world.

If you own or run a small to medium-sized business, *The Business Rules* is essential reading.

ISBN: 978 0 7499 2626 7